THE
LANE END

An Early R
in the Staffordshii   otteries

by
Rowan Patel

This view of May 1967 is looking down the route of the Lane End line towards the Trent & Mersey Canal. The standard gauge railway leads to Stoke Works and was built alongside the plateway when the Biddulph Valley line was constructed. To the left of this a cobbled surface may be seen passing beneath the bridge. This is the remains of the plateway and the cobbles formed the horse path between the rails.

Courtesy Allan C. Baker

THE OAKWOOD PRESS

© Rowan Patel, 2019

ISBN 978-0-85361-538-5

Printed by
Claro Print, Unit 2, Kirkhill House, 81 Broom Road East, Glasgow, G77 5LL

Looking west towards the canal, showing the bridge which once carried the North Staffordshire Railway (NSR) main line over the plateway. Stoke Works can be seen in the distance. *Courtesy of Grahame Boyes*

Front cover: A fine view of Pratts' Sidings signal box and the track which follows the route of the Lane End line, looking west towards the canal in 1971. The rails remaining from the re-laid section of the plateway are clearly visible to the left of the track.
Courtesy of Mike G. Fell

Published by
The Oakwood Press, 54-58 Mill Square, Catrine, KA5 6RD
Telephone: 01290 551122   Website: www.stenlake.co.uk

Contents

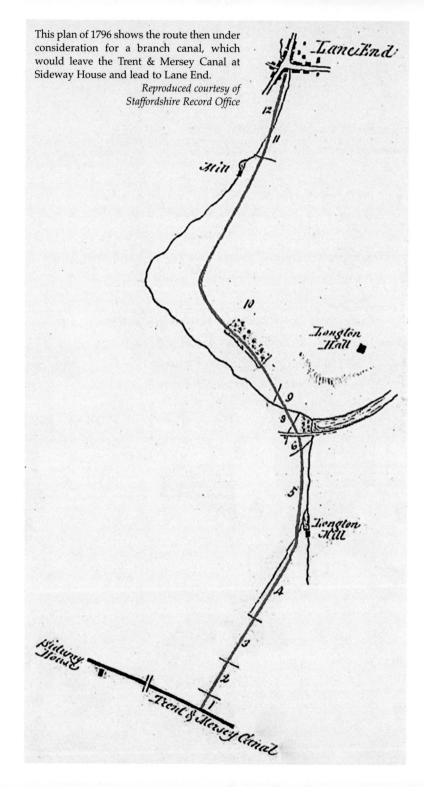

This plan of 1796 shows the route then under consideration for a branch canal, which would leave the Trent & Mersey Canal at Sideway House and lead to Lane End.

Reproduced courtesy of Staffordshire Record Office

Preface and Acknowledgements

Early railways constructed by canal companies for public use are full of interest and much has been written on this fascinating subject. Not far distant from Stoke-on-Trent, the railways of the Derby Canal Company, Peak Forest Canal Company and Ashby-de-la-Zouch Canal Company, to give but a few examples, have been much studied. The Trent & Mersey Canal Company's railways in the Staffordshire Potteries, of which the Lane End line was the longest, date from only a few years after these more famous lines.

My interest in the Lane End Plateway was triggered by the recovery of some track components, excavated during building work on the route of the line, over the course of which I kept a watchful eye in case anything should be uncovered. I soon wished to know the history of the route of which these artefacts formed a component, but rapidly realized that little had been written on this intriguing railway. Surprisingly the Lane End line has hitherto not even been the subject of an article, yet the railway is certainly not lacking in interest, as the following investigations hopefully demonstrate.

This book is the culmination of research beginning in November 2016, the same month that I first obtained a stone sleeper from the Lane End line. I am not a native of Staffordshire, for having grown up on the Wirral Peninsula, I moved to Stoke-on-Trent only in 2015. I was immediately intrigued by the unique landscape of the Potteries, so rich with the relics of the industry which gave the region its name. The opportunity to study the history of this area has been a pleasure. Much of my research has been conducted amongst primary sources and I am very grateful to staff at the numerous record offices and libraries where this material is held, namely Staffordshire Record Office, Derbyshire Record Office, Cheshire Record Office, the National Library of Scotland, Keele University Library, the Parliamentary Archives, the William Salt Library, Stoke-on-Trent City Archives and The National Archives.

I am also deeply indebted to a number of individuals who have been unstinting with both their time and their knowledge. Everybody that I have communicated with has been extremely generous in sharing their own research and this book has greatly benefitted from their experience and advice. Allan C. Baker, Richard Dean, Peter Lead, Michael Lewis and Andy Guy have all been kind enough to read and comment upon a draft of the whole book, whilst further help and valuable information has been provided by Grahame Boyes and Basil Jeuda. I would like to express my sincerest gratitude to them all.

Many of the archives and individuals mentioned have also helped by allowing me to use illustrations from their collections. I would also like to acknowledge the assistance of Mike Clarke and Peter Brown of the Railway and Canal Historical Society, the British Newspaper Archive, Staffordshire Past Track and Britain from Above, for supplying further illustrations. Lastly, thanks to my employer James Kent (Ceramic Materials) Ltd of Fenton, who allowed me to examine relevant documents on site and to salvage the artefacts found during building developments at my workplace. It was the recovery and conservation of these items which piqued my interest in the Lane End Plateway. The survival of these relics is fortunate indeed, for this railway has made for a fascinating and absorbing subject of study. Attempting to piece together and write its history has been a real privilege.

Rowan Patel,
Stoke-on-Trent, Staffordshire
June 2018

A view of the re-laid section of the Lane End line, looking east towards City Road in the early 1950s. The bridge visible to the left carries that road over the Biddulph Valley line.
Courtesy of Stoke-on-Trent City Archives

Terminology

When this line was constructed, shortly after the turn of the 19th century, it was always called a 'railway'. It terminated in the town of Lane End, hence it became known as the 'Lane End Railway'. Times change and a horse-drawn system such as this ceased to fit the popular definition of a railway even whilst it was in use. At this point it began to be called a 'tramway' and its name then started to be given as the 'Lane End Tramway'. The settlement of Lane End where the line ended was adjacent to another area called Longton, yet in time Lane End also became known as Longton and the former name fell entirely out of use. For this reason, in its final years, the line was sometimes known as the 'Longton Tramway'.

The terminology of early railways is confusing, with many similar terms in use to describe various early lines. I have referred to the Lane End line using only two terms. Firstly, I refer to it throughout this book as a 'railway', for that is undoubtedly what it was. Secondly, I have called it a 'plateway'. This is a term for a specific type of railway, where flanged rails of 'L' section are used with flangeless wheels. These flanged rails are known as 'plate rails'. I believe that to distinguish that this line was a plateway is important. Technically speaking, plateways were a very different system to that used today, where flanged wheels run upon flangeless rails. Finally, the name I have used for the line itself is the 'Lane End Plateway'. The railway never went by this name when in use. However, the names which were used, 'Lane End Railway' and 'Lane End Tramway', today have other meanings which tend to suggest something different to the type of transport system this plateway actually was.

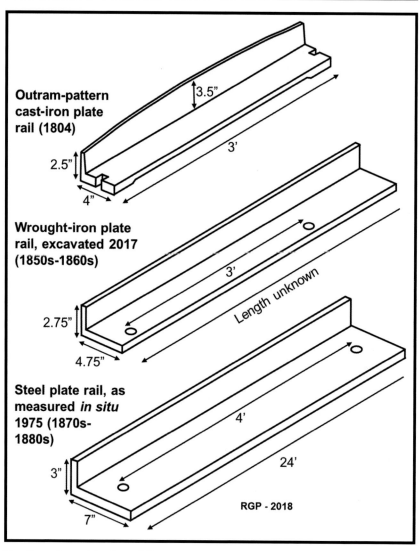

Outram-pattern cast-iron plate rail (1804)

3.5"
3'
2.5"
4"

Wrought-iron plate rail, excavated 2017 (1850s-1860s)

3'
Length unknown
2.75"
4.75"

Steel plate rail, as measured *in situ* 1975 (1870s-1880s)

4'
24'
3"
7"

RGP - 2018

The dimensions of the three different types of plate rail known to have been used on the Lane End line, from the cast-iron Outram-pattern rails used in 1804, through to rolled wrought-iron and steel sections used in later years.   *Author*

Introduction

This company was also empowered under an Act of 1802 to make railways in the Potteries and take tolls on them. Under it three lines totalling nearly five miles were built.   Bertram Baxter, *Stone Blocks and Iron Rails* (1966).

During its promotion, the scheme for the Trent & Mersey Canal received much enthusiastic support in the pottery towns of Staffordshire. For the transit of raw materials to the pottery factories, and for efficient carriage of the fragile ware to customers, a good transportation system was essential. The canal south of Stoke was opened by October 1772 and the route throughout was opened in May 1777. The Potteries blossomed as a result of the canal, indeed the number of pottery workers in North Staffordshire more than doubled between 1760 and 1785. The canal became the main artery of the Potteries. Its importance to the industry is obvious from the fact that between June and September 1783, more tolls were collected from the carriage of earthenware than from any other class of goods. The second largest source of revenue for the canal company was from carrying the potters' raw materials.[1]

Despite the numerous advantages offered by the canal, the centres of population where pottery manufacture flourished remained isolated from the canal system. Very few potteries adopted positions alongside the Trent & Mersey Canal, which was restricted to the valley of the Fowlea Brook. The traditional pottery towns of Longton, Fenton, Hanley, Burslem and Tunstall were all situated on land above and to the east of this stream. These towns were sited near to coal measures from which 'long-flame' coal could be obtained. This coal was ideal for the firing of ware, and anything between five and twelve tons of coal could be required for every ton of clay. Coal was not to be found near the canal, thus to keep down fuel transport costs, pottery factories largely remained near to the coal measures.[2] The canal became increasingly important for the import of raw materials and export of finished ware. However, for potteries based in the traditional pottery towns, a mile or more of rough and hilly roads separated them from the waterway. This was clearly less than ideal for the transport of such delicate goods. For the canal companies, to reach these towns was to tap an obvious source of revenue.

One North Staffordshire town long-associated with pottery manufacture was Lane End, this being nearly synonymous with modern-day Longton. Lane End and Longton were formerly separate townships adjoining one another, but the former name has now fallen out of use. The Trent & Mersey Canal Co. built a horse-drawn railway in 1804, linking Lane End to the canal. Although the remaining evidence of this early railway is slight, it was a very important route in its day. On completion, it was amongst the very first and was certainly the longest railway to have then been built in what now constitutes the city of Stoke-on-Trent. This book aims to study this interesting line. It is an examination of both its history and to a lesser extent its archaeology, as revealed by some items of permanent way recently excavated on its route.

NOTICE IS HEREBY GIVEN,

THAT application is intended to be made to Parliament in the next Seffion, for a bill to alter, explain and amend an Act paffed in the fixth year of the Reign of his prefent Majefty, intitled " An Act for making a Navigable Cut or Canal from the River Trent, at or near Wilden Ferry, in the county of Derby, to the River Merfey, at or near Runcorn Gap" —and alfo another Act paffed in the tenth year of the Reign of his faid Majefty, intitled an act to amend the faid act of the fixth year of the Reign of his prefent Majefty, for making the faid Cut or Canal, and for granting further powers for that purpofe—and alfo another act paffed in the fixteenth year of the reign of his prefent Majefty, intitled an act to enable the Company of Proprietors of the faid Navigation to make a navigable Canal from the faid Navigation on the fouth fide of Harecaftle to Froghall, and a Railway to Caldon Low, in the faid county of Stafford, and other Railways—and alfo another act paffed in the twenty-third year of his faid Majefty's reign, to amend and render more effectual the faid feveral former acts, and alfo to enable the Company of Proprietors of the faid Navigation to make a Railway from the faid Canal at Etruria to Shelton, Hanley, and Cobridge, another Railway from the faid Canal at Stoke upon Trent to Lane Delph & Lane End, another Railway from the faid Canal, or from a branch thereof, near Burflem, to the town of Burflem, and which faid Railways will pafs through or lie within the feveral townfhips or liberties of Etruria, Shelton, Hanley, Cobridge, Stoke upon Trent, Great Fenton, Little Fenton, Lane End, and Burflem, and in the feveral parifhes of Stoke upon Trent and Burflem, in the faid county of Stafford; and alfo to alter and vary the line of the prefent Railway from the faid Canal at Froghall, to the Lime Stone Quarries on Caldon Low, in the faid county of Stafford, and which lies within the feveral townfhips or liberties of Kingfley, Alveton, and Checkley, in the faid county. ·

THOS. SPARROW,
Clerk to the Company.

In the *Staffordshire Advertiser* of 6th September, 1800 the Trent & Mersey Canal Co. advertised their intention to build railways into the towns of the Potteries, including a line to 'Lane Delph and Lane End'.

CHAPTER ONE

Early Canal Schemes in the Pottery Towns

One of the earliest schemes to link the eastern pottery towns into the wider canal network, was proposed not by the Trent & Mersey Canal Co., but by a rival and ultimately unsuccessful scheme named the Commercial Canal, which first announced its plans late in 1795.[1] The planned route of the Commercial Canal passed through the Potteries at a higher level than the Trent & Mersey Canal, thus giving the potential for better access to the pottery towns, whilst breaking the monopoly of the Trent & Mersey Canal Co. The proposal, as advertised in August 1796, was for a canal which would begin at the Ashby-de-la-Zouch Canal in Ashby Woulds, Leicestershire and run to the Chester Canal at Nantwich in Cheshire. It was suggested that the system should include – 'a Navigable Cut or Branch from the said intended canal to or near Lane Delph and Lane End, in the parish of Stoke-upon-Trent...also for making and maintaining another Navigable Cut or Branch, Rail Way or Stone Road...to a certain Colliery, or Coal Works, in the parish of Burslem and township or hamlet of Sneyd, called Sneyd Collieries'.[2]

At the same time period in September 1796, the Trent & Mersey Canal Co. first advertised their intention to expand their network deeper into the towns of the Potteries.[3] This plan involved the construction of three short branch canals. A plan and book of reference to cover these canals was deposited at the quarter sessions on 13th September, 1796; the survey was carried out by Thomas Yates and William Cross (*see page 4*). The proprietors of the company made a petition to Parliament for the construction of these canals and an Act was duly obtained on 6th June, 1797. This authorized that a – 'Navigable Canal may be made...at Shelton, to or near Cobridge...at Longport, to a Place called Dale Hall, in Burslem...at a Place called Sideway House, near Stoke upon Trent, to or near Lane End...which said last-mentioned Canals will facilitate the Conveyance of Goods and Merchandize, and be of Public Utility'.[4]

The surviving book of reference shows that the lengths of these canals were planned as Lane End (1 mile 335 yards), Cobridge (1 mile 315 yards) and Dale Hall (585 yards). The plan showing the proposed routes of all three branches in 1796 indicates the final part of the route to Cobridge, not as a canal, but as a railway.[5] Ultimately however, the Parliamentary Act authorized a canal for the whole route, with no mention of a railway.[6] In likelihood the proposals must have been changed after the submission of the original Bill, such that this railway was no longer included. A revised plan for the canals as authorized by the 1797 Act is not known to have survived. In 1797 the canal company planned the route of another short railway which would adjoin the branch canal to Dale Hall, Burslem. This line ran 655 yards to Sneyd Colliery and there was a branch of 375 yards to Hot Lane in Burslem.[7] These railway schemes did not progress and no Act for their construction was ever obtained. The 1797 Act emphasized that the petitioners were willing and eager to build these three branch canals, yet the scheme did not come to any immediate fruition. The Burslem branch was constructed eventually, but it was not opened for another eight years.

In September 1797 a new route to Lane End was proposed, beginning at Froghall and involving a canal and railway.[8] This scheme may have been a further proposal of the Trent & Mersey Canal Co. The canal was to stretch from Froghall to Meir, a distance of some seven miles. The final mile from Meir to Lane End was to be a railway, so the railway formed an integral part of the route. A surviving estimate by civil engineer William Jessop (1745-1814) places the cost of the scheme at £44,861, of which 'One Mile of Iron Railway from Meer to Lane End' accounted for £1,500.[9] This plan would doubtless have allowed for efficient carriage of lime, coal and potters' materials to Lane End. It also provided a direct link between Lane End and the Trent & Mersey Canal at Etruria. However, this connection involved negotiating all 18 miles of the Caldon Canal along with the newly proposed route. It could scarcely therefore have been a tenable way of exporting ware for the potters of Lane End, since Lane End and Etruria were only around 3.5 miles apart by road. Ultimately this plan proved to be an abortive one.

Having obtained Parliamentary permission in June 1797, there was a lack of haste to actually build branch canals to Lane End, Cobridge and Burslem. In part this was because, even though it was in the canal company's interest to reach these towns, the Act was also one of their retaliatory efforts, which aimed to quash the aforementioned Commercial Canal. This scheme posed a serious threat and the timing of the branch canal plans suggests that they were, partially, an act of retaliation.[10] The failure to begin construction is probably also an indication that, even whilst the Act was being obtained, an alternative plan was being devised by the canal company. The advice of famous Scottish civil engineer John Rennie (1761-1821) was sought on these branch canals and he examined routes to Lane End, Hanley and Cobridge in February 1797.

Rennie had been asked to advise on the construction of a canal to Lane End, however a number of options presented themselves to him.

He wrote his thoughts on the matter in a notebook recording his visit. He commented that the possibilities were 'for a small Canal with inclined planes – Lord Stafford's Steward is for Rail Roads & others are for a wide Canal. It is ultimately difficult to judge from these different opinions what is best to be done'. Rennie's main objection to the small canal with inclined planes was that the speed of descent down the inclines would be likely to 'break the ware in the Crates & as they are of large Dimensions 5 feet long & 3 feet wide they would not stow very well'. He considered that a rail road would suffer from the same issues, although not to such a great extent as 'the carriage or waggon moving with a smaller velocity cannot shake them [the crates] so much'. A large canal on the other hand, he considered to be 'very expensive', whilst with multiple locks required it could take 2.5 hours to reach Lane End.[11]

In examining a route to Hanley and Cobridge on the same day, Rennie considered that a branch canal could be made as far as Hanley, but the continuation to Cobridge should be built as a 'Rail Road'. Rennie was evidently not convinced as to the suitability of a branch canal even as far as Hanley. In a report on the matter later in 1797 he observed that a railway 'would form a quick and cheap mode of carrying goods. Indeed, I do not know a cheaper or better [mode], and, in my opinion, it might be substituted with great advantage for the branch canal in question. I have therefore to submit whether, as a matter worthy of the consideration of the proprietors, this branch might not be saved, and a railroad substituted in its place'.[12] Of his three possible ways to reach Lane End, Rennie also seems to have settled on a railway when he made his recommendations to the canal company. The company appear to have taken Rennie's opinion to heart, for they then devised a new plan to reach the pottery towns using a series of horse-drawn railways. By this date railways were well known as a cheaper substitute for canal branches. Their potential was certainly known by the Trent & Mersey Canal Co., given they had constructed their first railway to the limestone quarries of Caldon Low in 1778. This was the first railway using iron rails (albeit as a plating overlying wood) constructed using the authority of an Act of Parliament.[13]

The first evidence of this new scheme is a notice printed in the *Staffordshire Advertiser* (*see page* 10) of 6th September, 1800 by Thomas Sparrow, the Clerk to the Trent & Mersey Canal Co. The specified intention was to – 'make a Railway from the said Canal at Etruria to Shelton, Hanley, and Cobridge, another Railway from the said Canal at Stoke upon Trent to Lane Delph and Lane End, another Railway from the said Canal, or a branch thereof, near Burslem, to the town of Burslem'.[14]

Clearly these railways were planned to fulfil exactly the same function as the branch canals considered previously. Also in September 1800, a survey was completed by Thomas Yates for those lines to Hanley, Cobridge and Lane End.[15] Although a Bill was submitted to Parliament for these proposals, this did not proceed in that Parliamentary session. Instead the scheme was revised almost exactly a year later in September 1801 and a plan of that date shows the revised railways.

This new plan omitted the branch railway to Cobridge from the Hanley line. The plan also included details of a third railway to Burslem.[16] Of the three proposed railways, this one was the exception, for it did not adjoin the Trent & Mersey Canal itself, but connected to the Burslem Branch Canal as authorized in 1797. Application was made to Parliament and these railways were authorized by an Act of 15th April, 1802. It was stated that – 'by Surveys lately made, it appears that Railways may be extended from the said…Canal to Lane End, Hanley and Burslem…which will be of great Advantage to the extensive Manufactories of Earthenware established at those places'.[17] It is these three railways which all came to be built. Due to the poor survival of the Trent & Mersey Canal Co.'s records, details of these lines are scarce. However, it is certain that they were of great benefit to the Staffordshire Potteries. Indeed, they must have had a significant influence on the development of the towns to which they were connected.

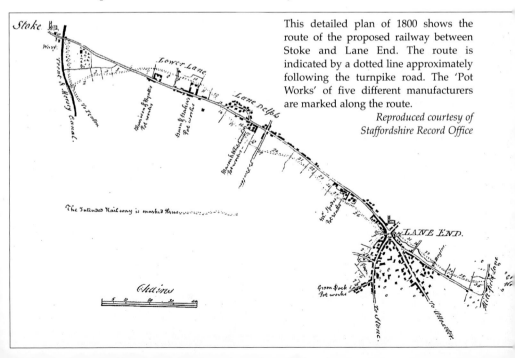

This detailed plan of 1800 shows the route of the proposed railway between Stoke and Lane End. The route is indicated by a dotted line approximately following the turnpike road. The 'Pot Works' of five different manufacturers are marked along the route.

Reproduced courtesy of Staffordshire Record Office

CHAPTER TWO

When were the 'Pottery Plateways' Constructed?

Unlike the branch canal proposals, the railways to the towns of the Potteries were constructed rapidly. Before looking at the construction of the Lane End Plateway, it seems prudent to briefly examine its sibling, the Hanley Plateway. This railway was already being constructed on 21st October, 1801, only a month after a revised survey was submitted to the quarter sessions on 23rd September, 1801. At this date a shop was advertised to let in the *Staffordshire Advertiser*. It was said that the shop's – 'situation is likely in a short time to be much improved by the Rail-way from Shelton Wharf, (which is now in great forwardness) passing in front of it'.[1] Since the Act of Parliament was not obtained until 15th April, 1802, the trackbed of this line was evidently being built at least six months before Parliamentary powers were obtained. Construction sounds to have been well advanced by October 1801. Presumably, since the line was quite short, any powers of compulsory purchase empowered by the Act were largely unnecessary and much relevant land had already been purchased by the canal company or wayleaves obtained. This railway seems to have been completed by 29th January, 1803. On this day several plots of land were advertised to be sold by auction in the *Staffordshire Advertiser*. It was said of two of these plots that – 'the lower part nearly adjoins the new railway',[2] which was evidently the Hanley Plateway.

There was local knowledge that a railway was to be built between Stoke and Lane End, even prior to the Act of 15th April being obtained. For instance, some days beforehand on 10th April, 1802, an advertisement was printed for – 'A complete set of Potworks...situated at Lane Delph, in the Staffordshire Potteries...The intended railway from Stoke Wharf crosses through a corner of the meadow : at a small expense a branch may be made to join the works'.[3] The railway had evidently not been finished on 21st January, 1804, when a property advertisement stated that – 'The new Railway from the Canal to Lane End, will pass close by the Garden'.[4] However, an advertisement dated 5th July, 1804 in the *Staffordshire Advertiser* then mentions – 'All that Water Mill for grinding Flint, situate at Lane-End called the Folley Mill, lately re-built, and the machinery entirely new; it is capable of doing much work, and lies within one hundred yards of the Railway from Stoke, from which to the mill is a very good road' (*see page 17*).[5] The evidence presented by these two newspaper advertisements seems a strong indication that the Lane End Plateway was opened to traffic between January and July of 1804. The construction of the line had probably begun at some point in 1803.

This advertisement for coal mines printed in the *Staffordshire Advertiser* of 9th March, 1803 states that the Lane End line was to be 'immediately made'.

© *The British Library Board and reproduced by permission of the British Newspaper Archive*

TO BE SOLD OR LET.

VALUABLE Mines of COALS, situated at Adderley Green, near Lane End, about two miles from the Grand Trunk Canal, at Stoke-upon-Trent, in the Staffordshire Potteries. The Land consists of about 48 acres and 1100 yards in length, in which there are three several mines, viz. the Adderly Green or Lawn Mine, being five feet thick, the Ragman, and the Seven Feet.

N. B. A railway is intended to be Immediately made from Stoke upon Trent aforesaid to Lane End, and near to the lands above mentioned.

For further particulars apply to Mr. RICHARD JOHNSON, of Lane End, Potter, or Mr. JAMES WRIGHT, near Burslem, Coalmaster.—A Purchaser may be accommodated with two-thirds of the purchase money.

9th March, 1803.

The Lane End line was by far the longest of the Trent & Mersey Canal Co.'s railways in the Potteries. As built it had a length of 2 miles 1,100 yards with a rise of 152 feet. At Lane End there was a side branch to Green Dock of 550 yards rising 25 feet. The Hanley Plateway was 1,485 yards long with a rise of 115 feet and had a side branch to Shelton of 165 yards.[6] At Burslem the canal company's plateway was not built until the Burslem Branch Canal was completed in 1805. The final route was still being surveyed late in 1810, for a diary entry of 10th October records that James Caldwell was 'at Burslem meeting Mr Robinson of Stone surveying the Ground and making arrangements relative to the Rail Road intended to be laid from the Wharf to the Town of Burslem'.[7] This line was the shortest of the three plateways, being a mere 605 yards in length and rising 86 feet, therefore it could probably have been built fairly quickly and must have opened in the early 1810s.

These railways were all the work of John Rennie, who having initially recommended their use rather than branch canals, was later appointed as their engineer.[8] He is well known for constructing the third Caldon Low railway, authorized by the same Act of 1802. However, Rennie is less well known as the engineer of these three canal plateways in the Potteries. The plateways were, without a doubt, amongst the first railways in the six towns of the Potteries. The only railway known which was definitely earlier, is a line at Burslem which was operating in October 1799, at which point it was still in the final stages of construction. This was a colliery line, carrying coal from local pits to the great pottery works of Enoch Wood.[9] It is not known whether this railway used plate or edge rails. The Hanley and Lane End plateways, completed by January 1803 and July 1804 respectively, were quite possibly the first railways ever built within the limits of the old parish of Stoke-upon-Trent.

It has been stated that small plateways were in use, for moving material around Spode Works by 1803. This date was carved on to a wagon used at Spode.[10] It is certainly the case that there was an internal plateway network at this pottery. This was connected to the Newcastle-under-Lyme Canal which ran alongside the Spode Works and opened in 1800. These plateways were probably built after the canal, but no other evidence has been found to qualify the date 1803, so it is not known if the system was genuinely this early. Similarly, there was an internal railway, almost certainly a plateway, in use at Wedgwood's factory at Etruria by 1814.[11] Narrow gauge plateways of a type used in Shropshire were imported to the North Staffordshire Coalfield by John Gilbert. He was using such a plateway between his pits at Kidsgrove and the Trent & Mersey Canal by 1797.[12] Any lines built in North Staffordshire up to 1804, however, had been relatively short. On construction the Lane End line was undoubtedly the longest railway ever built in the neighbourhood and it must have retained this distinction for some years. It is therefore an important route, which is of historic significance in the development of transportation within the Staffordshire Potteries.

To be difpofed of by Private Treaty,

THE under-mentioned valuable FREEHOLD ESTATES, the property of the late Mr. RI-CHARD MYATT, of Lane End, in the Potteries.

LOT I. All that fubftantial and well-built fet of Potworks, fituate at Lane End, called the Lower Works, moft advantageoufly fituated, being in the centre of extenfive collieries, clofe to the railway from the canal at Stoke, and conftantly fupplied with a ftream of foft water, conveyed into the Slip-houfe.

LOT II. All that Water Mill for grinding Flint, fituate at Lane-End, called the Folley Mill, lately re-built, and the machinery entirely new; it is capable of doing much work, and lies within one hundred yards of the Railway from Stoke, from which to the mill is a very good road; its fituation is very good, being clofe to manufaCtories, and the manner in which it is built being adapted for the addition of an engine, by which its powers may be increafed to a very great extent, and it is clofe to coals.

LOT III. Several Plots of building Land, fituate in Lane-End, in the Manor of Longton, in various fituations, well adapted either for private houfes or large faCtories.

LOT IV. Three commodious Pews, in the gallery of the church at Lane-End.

For further particulars and to treat for the fame apply to Mr. THOMAS NICKISSON, of Stone, Staffordthire.

Lane-End, July 5th, 1804.

The first evidence that the Lane End Plateway was operational is this advertisement for a flint mill dated 5th July, 1804, which highlights the existence of the railway as an advantageous feature in both lots I and II.

© *The British Library Board and reproduced by permission of the British Newspaper Archive*

A view of the remnants of the Lane End line behind Pratts' Sidings signal box *c.*1974.
Courtesy of Peter Lead

CHAPTER THREE

The Permanent Way of the Lane End Plateway

The plateways built by the Trent & Mersey Canal Co. to Lane End and Hanley were typical of those lines constructed on the principles of civil engineer and ironmaster Benjamin Outram (1764-1805). Angled cast-iron plate rails of 'L' section and three feet in length were spiked to blocks of stone. Outram had detailed this design of railway in his 'Minutes to be Observed on the Construction of Rail-ways', published in February 1801,[1] around six months before construction began on the Hanley line. The company's plateway to the limestone quarries of Caldon Low was built to the same plan. The plateway to Hanley seems to have been the first of these three lines to be built, whilst construction proceeded on the Lane End and Caldon Low plateways shortly afterwards. Outram was a partner in the famous Butterley Ironworks, which at this point was still trading under its earlier name as Benjamin Outram and Co. The rails for the Lane End Plateway were obtained from the Butterley Company, which at this time had a reputation for the supply of cast-iron rails, helped by the fact that Outram was both a founding partner and the leading plateway advocate of his day.

To purchase from Butterley may have been on the advice of John Rennie, who alongside being the engineer of the Trent & Mersey Canal plateways, had been involved in dealings with Butterley since the company's infancy in the 1790s.[2] Starting in July 1801, over a year before laying any rails began on these lines, Rennie was involved in the use of temporary plateways during the construction of London Docks. These lines used Butterley rails, so Rennie was already well acquainted with the products Butterley offered.[3] Rennie also ensured that Butterley's rails met his standards, when in May 1802 he carried out personal experiments, by applying a load to plate rails and testing them to breaking point.[4] He also took a professional interest in Outram's railway projects, for instance Outram sent Rennie information on the Peak Forest Canal plateway in 1801.[5]

Outram liked to have personal involvement in the plateways for which his ironworks supplied the rails, stating in 1798 – 'In works of considerable extent it is most agreeable to me to undertake the whole road to make by Contract'.[6] This was not the case on the Trent & Mersey Canal plateways. However, in May 1802 the London Dock Company paid the Butterley Company for 'forming, making & completing the Railways at the London Docks on Contract'.[7] Butterley themselves were contracted to form these plateways after Rennie recommended this to the London Dock Company. Since Rennie was the principal engineer of these docks, he must have observed first-hand Butterley's methods of forming these railways, after which Outram may have trusted his ability to successfully engineer other lines using his rails.

On 6th August, 1802 the Trent & Mersey Canal Co. entered into an agreement with the Butterley Ironworks stating that – 'The said Benjamin Outram and Company engage to make and provide for the said Company 16,000 Rails of cast iron to the pattern agreed upon. Each Rail to be 3 feet in length and to weigh on average 34 lbs. of the stoutest metal'.[8] Some seven weeks later the first batch of 2,344 'Gang Rails' were supplied to the canal company. This was the first of 13 instalments of cast-iron rails, generally supplied at approximately weekly intervals (*Table 1*).[9] The Butterley Company always described their cast-iron plate rails as 'Gang Rails', a gangway being a local term for a railway used only in the East Midlands. Along with some of the batches of gang rails supplied, the ironworks included other kinds of rail. For instance it supplied 230 'Road Rails', these being plates of a heavier section and incorporating a lower flange such that they could be used at level crossings. Also supplied were a number of 'Cross Rails' and 'Bevilled Rails' for use at plateway turn outs.[10] Butterley often supplied rails to canal companies with a guarantee of between one and three years that rails would be replaced, if broken in fair use.[11] The Trent & Mersey's rails are likely to have been covered by such a guarantee, although its duration is unknown.

Date	Item	Quantity	Rail Weight (lb/yd)
24th September, 1802	Gang Rails	2,344	33.9
	Road Rails	26	48.8
30th September	Gang Rails	1,200	33.4
7th October	Gang Rails	1,048	33.8
	Road Rails	84	49.0
13th October	Gang Rails	816	33.5
	Road Rails	72	49.3
20th October	Gang Rails	1,024	33.6
	Cross Rails	9	-
	Bevilled Rails	18	-
28th October	Three feet Gang Rails	1,296	34.0
8th November	Three feet Gang Rails	1,056	34.1
	Road Rails	48	48.0
20th November	Gang Rails	1,088	34.1

Date	Item	Quantity	Rail Weight (lb/yd)
27th November	Gang Rails	1,248	34.2
10th December	Gang Rails	1,246	33.9
20th December	Gang Rails	1,360	34.0
6th January, 1803	Gang Rails	1,360	34.0
8th February	Gang Rails	1,000	35.2

Table 1: Plateway rails bought from the Butterley Company by the Trent & Mersey Canal Co. in 1802-1803

By 8th February, 1803 the original contract for 16,000 rails had been fulfilled, a total of 16,104 gang rails then having been supplied. It seems probable that when they ordered 16,000 rails the canal company were placing an order with which they hoped to construct the lines to Lane End and Hanley. These two plateways would have required approximately 13,650 three foot plate rails between them. They were both single track railways, hence sufficient rails were also needed for passing places and as spares. Therefore 16,000 seems a reasonable number for the canal company's first rail order and they doubtless hoped to have a quantity of spare rails left over for use on their other lines. The rail weight per yard was susceptible to some fluctuation, but averaged across the order it was 34 lb/yd, exactly as requested in the original contract. The road rails supplied by Butterley were always heavier than the corresponding gang rails and in this instance they were 49 lb/yd. The castings were sold at £10 10s. per ton, hence with at least 10,500 rails necessary on the Lane End line it would have originally used over £1,600 worth of rails. To finish the order Butterley sold the canal company three batches of 'wheels & axles' between 23rd February and 24th March, 1803, for use in the construction of plateway wagons.[12]

At some point in 1804, the Trent & Mersey Canal Co. seem to have entered into a second contract with the Butterley Company, for the supply of further rails. No details of this agreement have survived, but the original furnace ledger shows that 11,747 gang rails were supplied between 3rd April and 19th October, 1804 (*Table 2*), this time at £11 per ton.[13] In the past it has been assumed that all the rails supplied by Butterley between 1802 and 1804 were for the Caldon Low Plateway. However, as explained it seems more likely that the original contract to supply 16,000 rails related to the Lane End and Hanley plateways. These two lines in the Potteries were built first, for at Caldon Low the company was able to use its pre-existing line of 1785 which the plateway would eventually replace. The rails supplied in 1804 on the other hand must

The Butterley Company's furnace ledger contains full details of the rails cast for the canal company between 1802 and 1804. These were used in the construction of three plateways.
Courtesy of Derbyshire Record Office, ref. D503/41/1

have been bought for Caldon Low. It has been shown that the Lane End line was completed by July 1804, yet many thousands of rails were still being bought after this date, for which the Caldon Low line was the only possible outlet.

Date	Item	Quantity	Rail Weight (lb/yd)
3rd April, 1804	Gang Rails	1,000	40.1
8th June	Gang Rails	1,100	38.2
14th June	Gang Rails	180	40.3
20th June	Gang Rails	961	38.1
5th July	Gang Rails	1,650	38.1
18th July	Gang Rails	1,200	8.4
19th July	Gang Rails	1,120	38.1
24th August	Gang Rails	470	37.8
8th September	Gang Rails	1,504	37.9
20th September	Gang Rails	1,382	37.8
19th October	Gang Rails	1,180	37.6

Table 2: Plateway rails bought from the Butterley Company by the Trent & Mersey Canal Co. in 1804

The rails purchased in 1804 were of a slightly heavier pattern, being on average something over 38 lb/yd. Having by this point experimented with 34 lb rails on their plateways in the Potteries, the canal company must have realized that a heavier weight was desirable at Caldon Low. They had previously constructed two other railways between Caldon Low and Froghall, completed in 1778 and 1785 respectively, so they were aware of the heavy traffic on this line. The company probably anticipated that this route would receive heavier use than the Lane End and Hanley lines, whilst their previous railways to Caldon Low had been less than satisfactory. They were therefore evidently keen to make the Caldon Low Plateway as durable as possible, by employing rails of a heavier weight.

The Caldon Low line is generally said to have been a double track plateway, on the authority of Farey who in 1817 described it as 'laid double'.[14] Although a double track line by this point, the rail quantities supplied by Butterley do not allow for this plateway to have been double throughout in the first instance. The Caldon Low line was some 3.5 miles in length and as can be seen from *Table 3*, the 38 lb rails supplied in 1804 accounted for only 3.3 miles of track. The shortfall could have been made up using rails from the original 1802-1803 order, of which there must have been some left over having built the Lane End and Hanley lines. As it was, when first completed in 1804, the Caldon Low Plateway was probably a double line only on the four self-acting inclined planes, with single track railway and passing places in between the inclines. If this was the case then the 28,081 rails supplied between 1802 and 1804 could have been used to build all three plateways, with an additional 2 per cent of the rails left over for use in passing places.

Sale Period	Item	Total Quantity Purchased	Equivalent Mileage	Average Rail Weight (lb/yd)
September 1802 – February 1803	Gang Rails	16,104	4.6	33.9
September 1802 – February 1803	Road Rails	230	0.065	48.8
April – October 1804	Gang Rails	11,747	3.3	38.4

Table 3: Details of all rails bought for the Trent & Mersey Canal plateways in 1802-1804

Surveys of 1803 reveal that on the plateways of the Ashby-de-la-Zouch Canal Co., engineered by Outram himself, the length of passing places and sidings amounted to 3 per cent of the mileage of the single track lines.[15] Therefore, the additional 2 per cent of rails left having built the Trent & Mersey Canal Co.'s three plateways, seems a reasonable figure to allow for passing places. All the same, this figure scarcely leaves room for there to have been any spare rails left of those supplied by Butterley. However, these are the only two rail orders placed with the Butterley Company by the Trent & Mersey Canal Co., and they never bought any further rails after October 1804. The canal company only ever bought railway goods such as rails and wagon wheels from Butterley. They must therefore have had one or more regular foundries, from which they already purchased any other items required on their canal network. Perhaps one of these foundries could offer a better price on 'Outram-pattern' plate rails. The company would rapidly have needed a stock of spare rails to cope with any breakages, so they must have had another supplier shortly after they stopped buying from Butterley. It could even be that the last rails used to complete the third Caldon Low line in 1804 came from a different source, since the Butterley-supplied rails end rather abruptly at an arbitrary value below 12,000 rails.

When they were first constructing their plateways, the canal company evidently turned to Butterley, based on both that ironwork's reputation for rails and on Rennie's recommendation. Having had unsatisfactory experiences on their late-18th century lines at Caldon Low, the canal company went to some lengths to ensure these railways were built to the highest standard. However, once the company had gained experience of plateways and their construction using Butterley rails, they went on to purchase further rails elsewhere. In the early 1810s, some years after completing the lines to Hanley, Lane End and Caldon Low, the company seem to have constructed their plateway to Burslem.[16] Rennie was also the engineer of this line,[17] but Butterley evidently did not supply the rails, which must have had another source. Many plate rails must also have been bought from another ironworks for the doubling of the Caldon Low line prior to 1817. The same foundry may have supplied those rails which would have been needed to maintain the Lane End and Hanley lines. There certainly seem to have been local Staffordshire ironworks producing plate rails prior to 1810. The rails used on local plateways at Woodhead in 1809 and Consall in 1815 were of Outram's pattern, but had not been supplied by the Butterley company.[18]

CHAPTER FOUR

An Archaeological Examination of the Permanent Way

Alongside the cast-iron rails, plateways built to Outram's principles required stone blocks to form the sleepers and wrought-iron spikes to affix the rails. These items were rarely supplied by the Butterley Company unless they were building the entire line under contract.[1] Each cast-iron plate had a square notch in the end, such that two consecutive rails when butted together, formed a hole into which a spike was hammered. The stone sleepers were drilled with a central hole and into the hole an oak plug was inserted to receive the spike. It is not known where the Trent & Mersey Canal Co. quarried the sleepers used at Lane End. However, building work on the line of the railway in 2016 and 2017 uncovered a number of stone blocks, two of which were recovered by the author. One of these is of a fairly coarse gritstone, whilst the other is of a finer grained sandstone, so the sleepers were obviously sourced from a variety of locations. These sleepers must date from the earliest incarnation of this plateway and date from 1803-1804. They are typical of the stone sleepers pioneered by Outram.

The permanent way of the Lane End Plateway. In the background two stone sleepers recovered from the route support an Outram-pattern plate rail of the type which would have been used on the line. In the foreground is the section of wrought-iron plate rail which was excavated with the sleepers. *Author*, scale: 12 inch rule

The upper surface of one sleeper has roughly broken away, although the remains of an iron spike are fused to the surface. It weighs 154 lbs and is therefore consistent with the weight of 150-200 lbs recommended by Outram in his 'Minutes' on railway construction. The second sleeper is in better condition, measuring 13 inches x 15 inches x 8 inches in depth. The central hole is 1.125 inches in diameter and 4 inches deep; it even contains the rusted flakes of an iron spike. Most interestingly the spike hole appears to have some highly corroded lead adhering to the top inside surface. Occasionally stone sleepers were plugged with lead, rather than the usual wooden plugs. It has previously been noted that the plateways at both Woodhead and Consall had some sleepers utilising lead plugs.[2] This confirms that this was a practice carried out on other lines in this area of North Staffordshire, although the reasoning behind it is unknown.

The author was also lucky enough to salvage a four foot section of wrought-iron plate rail in 2017, the only piece of rail discovered during the building excavations which uncovered the sleepers. This part of the railway, lying between Fountain and Manor Streets in Fenton, was out of use by the 1880s. The fibrous structure of the wrought-iron has been clearly exposed by decades of corrosion. This piece of rail weighs 17.5 lb/yd, which probably corresponds to a weight before corrosion of 20 lb/yd. Measured externally, the base of the rail is 4.75 inches across and the flange height is 2.75 inches with a wall thickness of 0.375 inches. The four foot section contains two circular holes, approximately 3 feet apart and some 0.875 inches in diameter. These do not line up with each other being around 0.5 inches out of alignment and have been rather roughly punched or drilled into the rail after the section was rolled.

It is not known if this wrought-iron rail would have been used in conjunction with stone sleepers. If the old sleepers were moved appropriately the same gauge could have been maintained. Interestingly, the wrought-iron rail discovered could not easily have been utilized in conjunction with the original cast-iron plates. The fact that this artefact was excavated on the main line suggests that the plateway may have, at least partially, been re-laid with wrought-iron rails. However, no other evidence of a re-laying is known on this section of the line. A short section of the plateway was re-laid at a late date, a point mentioned at the end of this chapter, but so far as is known there was no re-laying of the whole line. The presence of stone sleeper blocks means that permanent way dating from the earliest phase of the plateway was also present when the line closed. The fact that this rail is of wrought-iron suggests it is of an earlier date than if it was steel. When

The same items of permanent way, seen this time from the outside of the rails and facing towards the flange. On either end of the Outram pattern rail is the lug associated with a raised foot which was cast at both ends of these rails. *Author, scale: 12 inch rule*

This cast-iron plate rail made at Butterley was recovered from Codnor Park, Derbyshire. Rails of this kind would have been nailed down to the stone sleepers using wrought-iron spikes of the type shown. On the right-hand side of the rail the distinctive lug is clearly visible. *Author, scale: 20 pence*

For stone sleepers containing a single spike hole, as recovered from the Lane End line, the joints between plate rails were as shown. The square notches in the ends of each rail butted together to form a hole through which the rails were spiked down.

Author, scale: 20 pence

the Manchester, Sheffield and Lincolnshire Railway re-laid the plateway associated with the Peak Forest Canal around 1864, they used steel rails.[3] This artefact may date from the 1850s or 1860s.

No cast-iron plate rails from the Lane End line are known to have survived. This is barely surprising for the route of the plateway, which will be described in Chapter Six, has been so successfully built over that any existing evidence of the route is minimal. It has been stated by Peter Lead that there are surviving examples of the rails from the Caldon Low line.[4] There were very minor variations in the dimensions of the various plate rails produced by Butterley down the years, and those copied to the Butterley pattern by other foundries showed further differences. If a Butterley rail from the Caldon Low line did survive, this would clearly also show the exact form of the original Lane End rails. However, the author has unfortunately been unable to trace the location of any surviving plates from Caldon Low. Given these plateways were built so soon after the publication of Outram's 'Minutes' on railway construction, they probably conformed to the dimensions which he gave there:-

> The rails should be of the stoutest cast iron, one yard in length each, formed with a flanch on the inner edge about two inches and a half high at the ends, and three and a half in the centre; and shaped in the best manner to give strength to the rails, and keep the wheels in the track. The soles of the rails, for general purposes, should not be less than four inches broad; and the thickness proportioned for the work they are intended for. On rail-ways for heavy burdens, great use, and long duration, the rails should be very stout, weighing 40lbs. or, in some cases, nearly half an hundred weight, each. For rail-ways of less consequence less weight of metal will do; but it will not be prudent to use them of less than 30lbs. weight each.[5]

The most distinctive features of plate rails of Outram's pattern were a raised foot at the end of each rail, along with a half-hemispherical lug which increased rigidity. A fragment from the end of a plate rail flange, was found by the author in 2011 above Froghall, on the Caldon Low line's longest inclined plane.[6] This may well be part of one of the original rails ordered from Butterley and demonstrates the lug and foot so characteristic of Outram's design. The flange at the end of this rail was 2.5 inches in height and tapers from 0.5 to 0.625 inches in thickness. The base of the rail was 0.5 inches thick, but increases to 0.625 inches at the foot. Furthermore, a wear mark upon a stone block measured on the Caldon Low line, appears to have been left by a rail some 4 inches wide. From this fragment and wear mark, a fairly complete set of dimensions for a full rail can be deduced. These dimensions are exactly as specified in Outram's 'Minutes' and this probably means that the Lane End rails were cast to the dimensions published there.

There was a final phase of permanent way which has not yet been described and so far as is known this was only laid on the first 550 yards of the line leading from the canal. This section continued in use after the rest of the line had closed, a point which will be returned to in Chapter Nine. It was used by horse-drawn carts and the line was re-laid at a wider gauge to facilitate these vehicles. Very broad steel rails were used and some of these survived *in situ* in the late 1970s and possibly even into the 1980s. A number of photographs survive showing this section of the line. These show the rails to have been laid in setts with a cambered horse path in between them. In the 1950s Bertram Baxter measured the rails here to be 6.5 inches broad with a flange 2.25 inches tall, at which point they were spiked to wooden sleepers.[7] Further measurements were made by Peter Lead in 1975, who recorded rails with external dimensions of 7 inches wide and 3 inches tall, with a 0.5 inch wall thickness. The overall rail length was 24 feet, with the rails spiked down every four feet.[8] These rails were different to the wrought-iron section obtained by the author in 2017 and seem to date from a later period, possibly the 1870s or 1880s (*see page 8*).

Detail of the steel rails which were the last phase of permanent way on the Lane End line, they were laid between City Road and the canal, possibly in the 1870s-1880s.
Courtesy of Mike G. Fell

Further detail of the angled steel plate rails as seen behind Pratts' Sidings signal box in 1972. The setts between the rails formed a path for the horses.
Courtesy of Grahame Boyes

A full rail length can be made out on the left-hand side of the plateway, these steel rails were 24 feet long.   *Courtesy of Peter Lead*

Detail of the rails *in situ* near City Road and above the Biddulph Valley line c.1974. A spike can be seen at the end of the rail length. According to Bertram Baxter these rails were spiked to wooden sleepers.   *Courtesy of Peter Lead*

CHAPTER FIVE

Plateway Gauge and the Rolling Stock

The gauge first used on the Trent & Mersey Canal Co.'s three railways in the Potteries and also on the Caldon Low line was probably the same, but does not appear to have been recorded.[1] Outram's first plateways were built to a gauge of 3 feet 6 inches, but his favoured gauge later became 4 feet 2 inches. This was the gauge he recommended to others when he published his 'Minutes' on railway construction in 1801, stating – 'The best width of the road for general purposes is 4 feet 2 inches between the flanches of the rails'.[2] It would appear, however, that these canal plateways were built to Outram's earlier preferred gauge. The *Rules, Bye-laws, Regulations, & Orders* for the Trent & Mersey Navigation dated 1867 give details of the wagons permitted for use on the line, recording that – 'the wheels on each…axletree to be distant from each other three feet eight inches'.[3] This wheel gauge corresponds to a gauge of 3 feet 6 inches for the plateways themselves.

Two other pieces of evidence tend to corroborate an original gauge of 3 feet 6 inches at Lane End. Firstly, this gauge was used on the fourth Caldon Low railway of 1847, and the reason for this may be that it preserved the gauge of the plateway which preceded it. Secondly, the North Stafford Railway or Consall Plateway was built to this gauge.[4] This line was of virtually identical construction to the Trent & Mersey Canal plateways, which seem to have been a source of inspiration for its builders. This was particularly the case with the Lane End line, which the North Stafford Railway Company originally hoped might be connected to their line, a subject which will be raised in Chapter Eight. Clearly, their ambition to connect the two routes would be simplified if they built their line to a common gauge. When compared to lines in neighbouring counties, the Lane End line represents a late use of the 3 feet 6 inch gauge on an Outram-type plateway. Even as early as 1799 Outram himself was recommending a gauge of 4 feet 2 inches to the Ashby-de-la-Zouch Canal Committee.[5] The plateways which Butterley contractors built for Rennie at London Docks may have been of 3 feet 6 inch gauge. If Rennie was happy with these plateways, perhaps he felt satisfied that this gauge would also be suitable for the Trent & Mersey Canal lines.

As a public line, the wagons used on the Lane End Plateway must generally have been privately owned by those that paid tolls and utilized the line. The original Act of 1802 stipulated that the railway was for the 'Passage of Waggons and Carriages, of Forms and Constructions,

On this section of the North Stafford Railway to the south of Consall Lane, a length of stone sleeper blocks remain *in situ*, some of which now support a water trough. The erosion of the trackbed from around the sleepers has left many of the blocks exposed. This 2015 view provides a good illustration of the way the Lane End line would have been constructed, with the sleepers laid at the same gauge.   *Author*

and with Burthens suitable for such Railways, to be approved of by the said Company'. It was also a requirement for those using the line – 'That the Owner or Owners…of every Waggon or other Carriage…passing upon the said…Railways…shall cause his, her or their Name or Names, and Place or Places of Abode, to be painted in large White Capital Letters, and the Number of such…Waggon or Carriage, in Figures on some conspicuous Part of the Outside'. Any user failing to do this was liable for a fine of between 40s. and £5.[6]

Some information on the limits imposed on wagons in the latter days of the line may be gleaned from the Bye-laws of 1867. Wagons were to weigh no more than 0.5 tons and their maximum gross weight was 2.5 tons, hence no more than 2 tons could be carried per wagon. These weights could be checked, for it was a requirement of using the line that any haulier should 'when required, permit his wagon and loading to be weighed'. The dimensions for the plateway wagons were given as 6 feet in length and 5 feet 6 inches in width, whilst the axletrees were to be between 3 and 4 feet apart. Fines were imposed if these figures were not adhered to for – 'Any wagoner or other person who shall pass on the said Railways [Lane End and Hanley]...with any wagon or other carriage of any other size or dimensions, or with a greater weight of loading...shall forfeit and pay for every such offence a sum not exceeding forty shillings nor less than twenty shillings'.[7]

For plateway wagons of traditional construction the body of the wagon fitted in between the wheels, hence the width was limited by the plateway's gauge. Examples of such wagons exist from other canal plateways and these are probably representative of the wagons used on this line in its early years. The dimensions given in the Trent & Mersey Bye-laws suggest that in later years, wagons were used where the body of the wagon overhung the wheels. These figures are probably only the maximum permissible dimensions though, so more traditionally proportioned plateway wagons may also have remained in use.

Artefacts from the Caldon Low line may be able to shed some light on the wagons used on the Lane End route, at least up until the 1840s when the Caldon Low Plateway ceased to operate. As previously quoted, the 1802 Act stipulated that any wagon used at either Lane End or Caldon Low was to be built to a form approved by the canal company, with the loading regulated to a quantity suitable for the railway. The wagons used at Caldon Low were entirely owned by the canal company, since it was they who worked the Caldon Low limestone quarries. Therefore, at Caldon Low the wagons must have conformed to the canal company's self-imposed specification. At Lane End on the other hand, a wide range of wagons must have been employed, since the rolling stock was largely owned by the hauliers who paid tolls to use the route. The canal company did also keep a variety of wagons which were used on the plateway to Lane End for its own purposes. At a meeting of the Trent & Mersey Navigation Traffic Committee in 1854 'a Waggon and Horse for the Longton Tramway were ordered to be purchased'.[8]

A curved fragment of cast-iron found on the Cotton inclined plane at Caldon Low in 2015, is only 3 inches long, but certainly appears to be part of a plateway wagon wheel. This wheel was only 1 inch in width on the tread and 0.75 inch in thickness. The curvature matches perfectly, that of a fragment of wagon wheel in the author's possession from the Peak Forest Canal plateway. This is from a type of wagon used on that line after 1833, on which the wheels were 18 inches in diameter. The wagon wheels at Caldon Low may therefore have been of a similar diameter. The Peak Forest line used wheels of a more substantial section, some 1.5 inches wide by 1 inch thick, and wheels of this tread width were also used on the Derby Canal Railway.[9] This fragment from Caldon Low is therefore of lighter weight than those wheels used on similar canal plateways, yet elsewhere some plateway wagons had wheels as narrow as 0.375 inches, so this width was evidently viable.[10] A second fragment of wheel rim from the same incline varies very slightly in thickness, but confirms the use of wheels with a tread width of 1 inch. The Caldon Low line received heavier use than the Lane End line and its wagons would have necessitated a stronger build; therefore, in likelihood the early plateway wagons at Lane End used similarly light duty wheels something under 20 inches in diameter.

It has already been noted that the dimensions of the wagons used at Lane End by 1867, do not seem to have been of traditional plateway vehicle construction. Similarly, the 1867 Bye-laws state in relation to the wagons wheels that – 'The tire [is] to be convex, and of the breadth of three inches, with nails countersunk'.[11] The 3 inch wide wheels referred to were clearly not cast-iron. The fact they were of nailed construction suggests they were wooden, perhaps with an iron 'tire'. These wheels seem to have been more akin to cart wheels than cast-iron flangeless wheels for railway use, such as the fragments from Caldon Low. At this date the Lane End line was operated by the North Staffordshire Railway (NSR), a matter which will be discussed in Chapter Nine. It appears that in these later years wagons of an entirely different construction were used, to those which might have been used in earlier years. Use by cart-type vehicles at an even earlier date is suggested by a plan and section for the proposed Biddulph Valley railway dated 1853. This included details for a short railway branch running alongside the plateway, which was 'To be passed alongside the present Cart Tramway, level unaltered'. The term 'Cart Tramway' certainly seems to imply some use by carts rather than plateway wagons in 1853.[12]

CHAPTER SIX

The Route of the Line

The proposed route of this railway is shown very well by Thomas Yates' plan dated 1800 (*see page 14*), however the route as built seems to have exhibited minor deviations from the original plan. The 1802 Act stated that deviations to the submitted plans could be made, so long as the permission of the relevant landowners was obtained.[1] The Trent & Mersey Canal Co. prepared a survey of their entire system in 1816. This devoted three pages to the Lane End line and shows the route in considerable detail.[2] The earliest published map showing the railway is Thomas Hargreaves' *Map of the Staffordshire Potteries* of 1832.[3] This map post-dates the line's opening by almost 30 years, yet it is probable that there were few major changes in those decades, for the route between Stoke and Lane End was still fairly rural (*see page 56*). The course of the railway will now be described as indicated by both the 1816 survey and Hargreaves, whilst the route will be related to today's landscape.

The Lane End Plateway began at a canal basin at Whieldon's Grove, off Whieldon Road, Stoke-upon-Trent. This basin was a small rectangular cut off the main canal and was clearly shown on the 1816 survey. It had a narrow entrance which opened out into a wider body of water. Hargreaves shows the railway itself to have split at the basin,

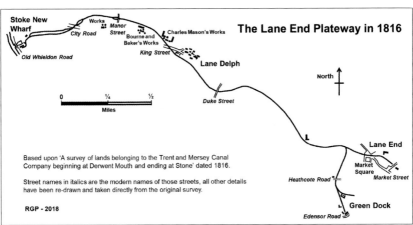

This map has been re-drawn from a wonderful survey commissioned by the Trent & Mersey Canal Co. in 1816. Interestingly only two passing loops are shown. Another intriguing feature is that the rails are not shown crossing Manor Street or Duke Street, possibly a sign that these were originally carried over the line on bridges. The railway ran through the edge of the Market Square in the very centre of Lane End   *Author*

A remarkable survivor as viewed from the west side of the canal in 2018, the bricked-up bridge No. 111 formerly passed over the entrance to Stoke Basin. This basin was built as the railway/waterway interchange where the plateway met the canal.   *Author*

with a branch passing down either side of the cut. Whieldon Road crossed the entrance to the basin by means of a humpback bridge and this was also shown in 1816. Remarkably this bridge still exists as bridge No. 111, although it has been bricked up on both sides. The basin itself has been entirely infilled and its site is now the premises of a haulage company. The entire bridge is extant within their yard, whilst the front of the bridge may be viewed well from the canal towpath. This relic forms a noteworthy survivor from the Lane End route.

From the basin the railway ran eastwards to cross the turnpike road from Newcastle-under-Lyme to Uttoxeter via a level crossing. The 1816 plan shows that the portion of the line between the canal basin and the turnpike was double track at that point, whilst the rest of the route was single track. The turnpike is now City Road and the route of the plateway may be seen to the south of that road, alongside the disused Biddulph Valley railway. The alignment takes the form of a track, still under railway ownership, which runs above the disused railway. Although inaccessible, this track still runs a large fraction of the way back to the canal. As viewed from City Road, one is struck by the very steep gradient as the route climbs up to meet the turnpike. On average the gradient of this railway was around 1 in 30. In later years the plateway between the basin and the turnpike was crossed by two bridges carrying the NSR lines to Derby and Stone.

The plateway ran just north of the turnpike road having crossed it. Its alignment there can currently only be traced as boundaries, for example the northern wall of the Stoke Workshops for the Blind. Eventually the line reached the town of Fenton, where it crossed a road now called Manor Street. East of Manor Street the route continues as the boundary

Famous historian of early railways Bertram Baxter took this photograph of the Lane End Plateway c.1939. The steep gradient of this section of the line is clear. The buildings visible are on the north side of City Road, previously the site of a level crossing.
Courtesy of The Railway & Canal Historical Society, Baxter Collection

In this view of the Lane End line, which probably dates from the 1950s, the angled plate rails are plainly evident. The kiln visible in the distance was associated with the Devon Pottery of S. Fielding & Co., based in Sutherland Street. The railway yard on the right is Pratts' Sidings.   *Courtesy of Stoke-on-Trent City Archives*

Looking west along the trackbed of the Lane End line in 2018, from City Road down towards the canal. The route is now a track above the disused Biddulph Valley line which lies to the right.   *Author*

A 2017 view, looking east up the trackbed to City Road, which was formerly the turnpike road between Stoke and Lane End. It was at this location that steel plate rails remained *in situ* throughout the 1970s.   *Author*

Having crossed to the north side of City Road the plateway ran alongside and above the Biddulph Valley line. In 1972 the old trackbed could still be discerned as wide strip of land, seen here at the end of Herbert Street and looking north. The alignment is now covered in housing at this point.   *Courtesy of Grahame Boyes*

wall between a primary school and the premises of ceramic materials manufacturer James Kent (Ceramic Materials) Ltd. Having crossed this factory site the route of the plateway follows the road Hitchman Street. The line then crossed back to the south side of the turnpike, present day King Street, and ran to an area which Hargreaves called 'Lane Delph'. At Lane Delph it crossed over present-day Duke Street, to run approximately parallel to the turnpike road.

Most of the roads on the route of this railway seem to have been crossed by level crossings. The 1816 survey shows the route passing over some roads in this manner. However, it is interesting to note that at both Manor Street and Duke Street, the line of rails clearly stops on reaching the roads, only to continue on the other side. At Manor Street there was a passing place in 1816, both lines of which disappear, only to be indicated again on the other side of the road. This seems to imply that there were once bridges over the line on these two roads, although Hargreaves shows no bridges and drew the line crossing all roads on the level. To the west of Duke Street the appropriately named road 'Old Tramway' preserves the alignment, although nothing from the plateway's era can be seen in the vicinity today.

The road Hitchman Street as seen looking west in 2018. This follows the old route of the plateway in this part of Fenton. At the end of the road is the chimney stack of James Kent (Ceramic Materials) Ltd, the factory of which is intersected by the former route of the line.
Author

The road off Duke Street known as 'Old Tramway' and now a dead end was previously longer, with a path utilizing the route of the line and leading to King Street. This view *c*.1939 looks south along this path towards pottery works in Duke Street.

Courtesy of The Railway & Canal Historical Society, Baxter Collection

The aptly named road 'Old Tramway' preserves the alignment of the railway up to Duke Street, where there was formerly a level crossing. This photograph looking north-west shows the road in 2018. *Author*

Urbanization has covered the route of the Lane End line. There are now few reminders that this railway was once such an important feature of this part of the Potteries. This road name is a notable exception.   *Author*

Having crossed Duke Street the plateway paralleled the south side of the turnpike. The land remained primarily undeveloped here in 1832 and no more roads or other features were intersected on Hargreaves' map. The site of the line here scarcely relates to any present-day land features, other than a short section which coincides with Oldfield Street. On reaching Lane End the plateway diverged into two separate branches; one of these ran down Market Street, the second to a point on Edensor Road then known as Green Dock. Formerly the alignment of this branch to Green Dock was preserved as two roads, Cooke Street and Corwell Road. However, these have now long since been destroyed by the construction of the A50 dual carriageway. The 1816 survey shows how the main branch to Green Dock originally had a short sub-branch leaving it near the southern end. Of the branch to the other side of Lane End, Market Street was previously named 'High Street' and Hargreaves shows this branch running parallel to that road, a little to the north. This branch passed through the very centre of the town; indeed, the 1816 survey shows how it actually passed through the edge of the 'Market Square'. As an early urban railway, the plateway here must have been a conspicuous feature of the local scene.

This 1973 view shows the route of the line behind Longton station, which stands to the left. This is near the junction where two branches formerly diverged to different parts of the town. One branch continued straight on to pass alongside Market Street, the other turned right to reach Green Dock. *Courtesy of Grahame Boyes*

Corwell Road in Longton followed the route of the Lane End line's Green Dock branch, but it no longer exists. It is seen here looking north in 1973. In the distance the kilns and chimney of the Albion Works are still standing today. *Courtesy of Grahame Boyes*

Another road which no longer exists, but which preserved the alignment of the branch line to Green Dock, is Cooke Street. This view of March 1973 is looking south towards Edensor Road. At the end of the street the kilns of the Elektra Porcelain Company can be seen.

Courtesy of Grahame Boyes

The branch to the potteries at Green Dock ended at a point on Edensor Road, which used to be opposite the end of Cooke Street. In 1973 the works of the Elektra Porcelain Company stood at the point this branch terminated. This was the site of Green Dock Pot Works when the line was first surveyed in 1800. *Courtesy of Grahame Boyes*

CHAPTER SEVEN

Operation, Customers and Materials Carried

The 1802 Act of Parliament authorized the Trent & Mersey Canal Co. to collect tolls for 'all Coal, Stone, Timber, and other Goods, Wares, and Merchandize, which shall be navigated, carried, or conveyed upon the said Railways'.[1] Since detailed financial records of the Trent & Mersey Canal Co. are no longer available, the revenue derived from tolls collected on this plateway cannot easily be assessed. The tolls charged were probably the same as those which applied on the canal itself, which in 1817 were 1*d*. per ton per mile, a value which remained unchanged in 1849. The maximum toll which could be applied on the canal was 1$^{1}/_{2}$ *d*. per ton per mile.[2] Restrictions on the maximum tolls permissible on the railway were enforced by the Act and were as follows:-

> For all Coal, Limestone, or other Stone, Sagar[s], Clay, Bricks, and Sand, to be carried or conveyed upon any of the said Railways so proposed to be made from the said first-mentioned Canal to Lane End, Hanley, and Burselm, any Sum not exceeding Two Pence per Ton per Mile, and for all other Goods and Merchandize any Sum not exceeding Three Pence per Ton per Mile.[3]

A section in the Act allowed fractional miles to be rounded up and down, such that a distance of over half a mile might be taken as one mile for the purpose of charging tolls. However, even though the Lane End line was to come to just over 2.5 miles, it was specifically forbidden for the length of this railway to be taken as three miles. The Act stipulated that – 'the said Railway from the Canal at Stoke to the Lower Market Place in Lane End aforesaid, shall, on calculating the said Rates on such Goods as shall pass on the said Railway to or from the said Market Place, be considered and estimated at Two Miles only'.

Goods on the canal were conveyed by private companies known as 'carriers'. Some of these companies also owned wagons and acted as hauliers on the canal company's railways. The canal company itself was a carrier for it owned the carrying firm Hugh Henshall & Co.[4] It seems probable that this company was involved in moving goods on the Lane End Plateway. At a meeting of the NSR Canal Traffic Committee in 1868 the 'Cartage Rates' to be charged to carriers using the canal company's railways were discussed. Tolls on the Lane End line had then increased somewhat above the amounts stipulated in the original Act. Carriage of earthenware was charged at the rate of 2*s*. per

ton per mile, due to the fragility of the cargo.[5] Other goods on the Lane
End line were to be charged as shown in *Table 4*.

Carriage To	General Goods (per ton)	Potters' Materials (per ton)	Calcined Bones and Bone Ash (per ton)
Stoke	1s.	1s.	9d.
Fenton	1s. 6d.	1s.	9d.
Lane Delph	2s.	1s.	1s.
Longton	2s.	1s. 6d.	9d.

Table 4: General cartage rates in 1868 for materials conveyed from the canal to settlements
on the Lane End Plateway.

The 1868 cartage rates in *Table 4* were reduced for works in Longton
which had 'railway accommodation'. Likewise, at a meeting in 1872 a
reduced toll of 1s. 3d. was agreed when conveying flint 'from Stoke to
mills and works in Longton having Railway sidings'. The companies
purchasing flint with sidings on the Lane End line were Bridgewood &
Son, Beech & Son, Longton Mill Co., Holland & Green and J. F. Wileman.
By 1873 the tolls to convey potters' materials, calcined bone and bone
ash, to Fenton and Longton had increased by between 2d. and 3d.
compared to in 1868.[6]

The Bye-laws of the Trent & Mersey Canal for 1867 have an entire
section devoted to operating practices for the 'Hanley and Lane-End
Railways'. Many of these rules had probably been in place for decades
by this point, for the rules to be observed when working the line seem
unlikely to have altered significantly. An earlier edition of the Bye-laws
printed at an unknown date after 1865, suggests that these particular
regulations may originally have been agreed at a meeting in 1833. The
speed at which the line could be worked was limited to 'the ordinary
walk of a horse', with a penalty of between 20 and 40 shillings for
leading the horse at a faster pace. The same fine applied 'If any wagoner
or other person shall sit or ride on any wagon or other carriage in going
up or down the said Railways'.[7]

A smaller minimum fine of five shillings applied should any of the
gates on the line be left open. It seems likely that most of these gates
were situated at the various level crossings. Another regulation related
to the use of passing places, here called turnouts. If going 'down' the
railway then the 'wagoner' had to pass through the turnouts, whilst if
going 'up' they were required to 'keep the Main Line'. It is not specified
which of the directions up/down was away from the canal and which
was towards the canal.

24 That all boats Navigating the said Navigation, and going northwards shall pass through the new Tunnel at Harecastle, and all such boats going southwards shall pass through the old Tunnel at Harecastle, under the penalty in each case on the person Navigating such boats of any sum of money not exceeding five pounds, nor less than forty shillings.

Hanley and Lane-End Railways.

25 That no wagon or other carriage but such as are of the following form and construction, shall be permitted to pass on the said Railways or either of them, viz :—

The fore and hind axletrees of such Wagon or other carriage, to be distant not less than three feet nor more than four feet, and the wheels on each such axletree to be distant from each other three feet eight inches.

The tire to be convex, and of the breadth of three inches, with nails countersunk.

The platform or chest to be of the length of six feet, and breadth of five feet six inches.

And no such wagon or other carriage to exceed ten hundred in weight.

26 Any wagoner or other person who shall pass on the said Railways or either of them with any wagon or other carriage of any other size or dimensions, or with a greater weight of loading than two tons ten hundred including such carriage, shall forfeit and pay for every such offence a sum not exceeding forty shillings, nor less than twenty shillings.

27 Every wagoner or other person shall, when required, permit his wagon and loading to be weighed, under the penalty of a sum not exceeding forty shillings, nor less than twenty shillings.

28 Every wagoner or other person in going down the said Railways or either of them, with any wagon or other carriage, shall pass through the Turnouts thereof, and in going up the same to keep the Main Line, under the penalty of a sum not exceeding forty shillings, nor less than twenty shillings.

The *Rules, Bye-laws, Regulations, & Orders, with Reference to the Navigation from the Trent to the Mersey* dated 1867 include a very rare set of operational regulations for the canal company's plateways. *Courtesy Collection Allan C. Baker*

29 Every person having the care of any wagon or other carriage, who shall suffer the same to pass on the said Railways or either of them, faster than the ordinary walk of a horse, shall forfeit and pay for every such offence a sum not exceeding forty shillings, nor less than twenty shillings.

30 If any wagoner or other person, either in going up or down the said Railways or either of them, shall leave open any of the gates thereof, he shall forfeit and pay for every such offence a sum not exceeding forty shillings, nor less than five shillings.

31 If any wagoner or other person shall sit or ride on any wagon or other carriage, in going up or down the said Railways or either of them, he shall forfeit and pay for every such offence a sum not exceeding forty shillings nor less than twenty shillings.

32 If any wagoner or other person, shall, in passing up or down the said Railways or either of them, suffer his wagon to pass over the tongues at the termination of the Turnouts, he shall forfeit and pay for every such offence a sum not exceeding forty shillings, nor less than twenty shillings.

33 That any boatman or person Navigating or using any boat, or other vessel, on the said Navigation or any branch thereof, shall, on passing up any lock with such boat or other vessel, at which there is a side pond, draw the water from such side pond, and shut down the paddles of such side pond before drawing the upper cloughs or paddles of such lock; and on passing down any such lock, shall draw as much water as possible into such side pond and shut down the paddles of such side pond previously to drawing the lower cloughs or paddles of such lock; and every person neglecting or omitting to draw the water in manner aforesaid, shall forfeit and pay for every such offence any sum of money not exceeding forty shillings, nor less than twenty shillings.

34 That no boat be permitted to pass through a lock on this Navigation in the absence of the Captain or person intrusted by the owner of the boat with the charge and care of the cargo on board.

Once in use, the plateway rapidly became a feature of advertisements in the *Staffordshire Advertiser*, always listing it as a benefit (*see page 58*). Some examples of these advertisements are well worth quoting, for they demonstrate what a useful asset the line must have been to local pottery factories, many of which must have begun to use the route as soon as it was completed:-

5th January, 1805
A...set of POT-WORKS...on which the Manufacture may be very considerably extended, situate at Folly, in Lane End aforesaid, adjoining the Turnpike Road, and the new Collieries, lately opened there and within 100 yards of the Railway leading from the Grand Trunk Canal, at Stoke, to Lane End.[8]

11th April, 1812
A Convenient set of POTWORKS, situate in Lane End, in the Staffordshire Potteries, fronting to the Market-place...There is a constant supply of water to these Pot-Works, which are also advantageously situated near to a railway leading from Lane End to Stoke.[9]

14th July, 1818
FLINT MILL, TO BE LET, Situate at Lane-End; containing Flint, Glaze and Colour Pans, close to the Railway from Stoke to Lane-End, and within a few hundred yards of the numerous manufactories in that place.[10]

A further advertisement of 1811 lists five 'newly erected Dwelling-houses', which are advertised one and two houses at a time, in three different lots. A fourth lot contained – 'A valuable Plot of Ground for building upon, adjoining the first three Lots, and containing 635 square yards or thereabouts'. It was specified that – 'The whole of the foregoing Lots adjoin the Turnpike Road between Lane End and Stoke upon Trent, and the first and fourth Lots possess the additional convenience of being immediately contiguous to the Railway leading to the Grand Trunk Canal'.[11] It is interesting to note that there was clearly a large amount of building work occurring in the neighbourhood. New houses, many of which were doubtless occupied by pottery workers, and also vacant land, were both in high demand. The Lane End Plateway must have played its part in further urbanizing and industrializing the towns through which it passed.

A contemporary description of the line in 1829 was given by Shaw in his *History of the Staffordshire Potteries*:-

From Stoke to Lane End they [the canal company] have a Rail Road, on which their Waggons regularly convey materials and packages to the neighbourhood of Fenton, Lane Delph, and Lane End: and return with any Crates, &c.[12]

A further description of the plateway in 1843 was given by Ward in his *The Borough of Stoke-upon-Trent*:-

> A Rail-road for horse-draft extends from Longton, through the Fentons, for the conveyance of the merchandise of those places, to and from a wharf and basin on the east side of the canal, near Stoke, where capacious warehouses are erected.[13]

The basin and warehouses at the point the railway met the canal are worthy of further discussion. The basin seems likely to have been constructed around the same time as the line itself, although interestingly the 1816 survey covered in Chapter Six marks it as 'Stoke New Wharf'. It went by the name of 'Stoke Basin' from at least as early as 1819, when it was mentioned in connection with the railway – 'Wanted a New 40 Horse Power Steam Engine, on the most improved plan...to be put up complete...within a mile of Stoke Basin, in the Staffordshire Potteries, from which there is a railway to the place where the engine is to be erected'.[14] The construction of a basin adjoining the canal itself allowed for substantial wharves and also for the erection of buildings serving the plateway. The warehouses were used by the carrying companies which made a business of moving goods on the plateway and canal. Evidence from maps suggests that this was a significant transport interchange, with what amounted to an early railway goods yard developed alongside the canal.

Hargreaves' map shows that by 1831 there were two buildings on the southern side of the basin. These warehouses are shown in more detail on a plan of 1853, by which point one had been extended to the full length of the basin. The two buildings were then rail-served, with a line passing between them, whilst three further lines diverged to the north of the wharf.[15] A small building, probably a weigh house, stood at the point the lines separated and this was also shown by Hargreaves. In the line's latter years the locomotive, carriage and wagon works of the NSR grew up to the north of the basin. These works were served by a standard gauge branch built at the same time as the Biddulph Valley line and running alongside the plateway. Even before the development of the NSR's Stoke Works, there was a large canalside building on the site they later occupied. This building, along with the warehouses and plateway lines at Stoke Basin, are shown on a plan of c.1856.[16]

Alongside its connection to the pottery industry, carrying raw materials and finished ware, the Lane End Plateway was also served by much colliery traffic. In the production of ware, up to 12 tons of coal were required for every ton of clay, hence much coal was destined to the

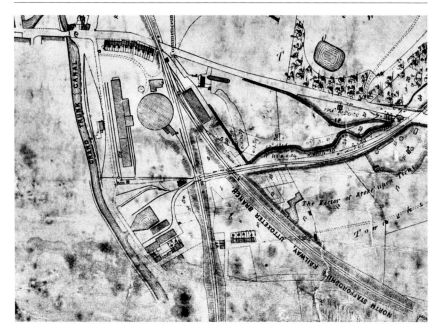

This plan *c.*1856 dates from the building of the NSR's Biddulph Valley line (its line of deviation shown curving away from the railway junction, then following a line immediately north of the plateway). It shows the trackwork and warehousing at Stoke Basin at that time.   *Courtesy of Richard Dean, Canalmaps Archive*

pottery factories which consumed vast quantities of fuel. In the early 1830s the line served a number of pits in the vicinity of Lane End, whilst coal was also extensively extracted in Fenton in the early 19th century.[17] It is probable that the plateway was associated with many local coal mines from shortly after opening. Indeed, the opening of the line doubtless triggered an expansion of the local coal mining industry. Hargreaves' map of 1832 shows several collieries directly on the line of the railway. Coal seams mined in the vicinity of Lane End were of a high quality, capable of quickly attaining high temperatures. These coals were especially suited to the firing of bone china, hence the manufacture of this kind of pottery became firmly established there.[18]

Many of the collieries would have maintained their own branch lines, to give them a direct connection with the Lane End line. An example is the Fenton Park Colliery which by 1804 was being worked by Josiah Spode II. Having used the Lane End line he could easily convey coal to his Spode Works using the Trent & Mersey and Newcastle-under-Lyme canals.[19] As early as 1806 another colliery was delivering coal to the

This fine photograph *c.*1900 looks up towards what is now City Road from the NSR's Stoke Works. The first bridge passes over the main line railway to Stone, whilst the second bridge in the distance carries the Derby line. These bridges were built to accommodate the Lane End Plateway, the remains of which can just be discerned in the background passing under the bridge on the right-hand side.

Courtesy Collection Allan C. Baker

works of Messrs Turner & Co, using its own branch to the Lane End line which led directly from the mine's entrance. This advantageous arrangement is described in the following interesting advertisement:-

> An old established and well accustomed Manufactory...where the making of Porcelain, & Earthenware, in all its branches, has been carried on to a great extent, for a great number of years. The Manufactory embraces advantages, seldom or ever met with in similar situations, in affording a never failing supply of Water, and the ready delivery of Coals, by a Railway, within 40 yards of the Pit's Mouth; even without the assistance of a Horse. The singular advantage in a consumption of 40 Tons of Coal per week, would render a direct saving of £150 per Anum. And as a Railway is now laid from Lane End to Stoke, the necessity of keeping a team of horses for this Manufactory will be completed obviated.[20]

Some of the colliery lines which developed in association with the Lane End Plateway were extensive. This is especially the case of a network which grew to serve numerous collieries on land standing above and to the north of Fenton. This network is shown both on Hargreaves' map and on the survey of Phillips and Hutchings,[21] both published in 1832. Neither of these maps marks a connection to the Lane End line, but the branch is shown to terminate a matter of yards from it, near the southern end of Victoria Road. From here it ran half a mile west to Fenton Park Colliery, connecting to several other pits such as Broad Fields Colliery along the way. From Fenton Park the line continued north for over half a mile to reach another mine. This system is also shown by the one-inch Ordnance Survey map of 1836 and this does mark a physical connection to the Lane End line. Another branch on this map began at Adderley House Colliery to the north of Lane End and ran to a point next to the Lane End line.[22]

The iron industry also used the Lane End Plateway, for example the Lane End Ironworks of William Sparrow were constructed alongside the line in 1824. Sparrow, an ironmaster from Wolverhampton, built this ironworks to smelt ironstone found in Plackett's Brook Colliery. The iron produced was conveyed along the plateway and was then taken to the Black Country by canal for further processing.[23] Coking coals and clayband ironstone suitable for iron production also outcropped at Fenton. These resources were exploited at Fenton Low at a similar time to Lane End, an ironworks being constructed there in the 1830s by Messrs. Thompson and Massie.[24] This ironworks stood north of the Lane End line and may well have benefitted from the efficient transport links it provided.

In 1829 the maintenance costs of the Trent & Mersey Canal's three pottery plateways stood at £157 4s. 9d., whilst their plateway from Froghall to Caldon Low cost £374 9s. 1d. to repair. This works out at repair costs of approximately £37 per mile in the Potteries and £107 per mile at Caldon Low. This is not to say that the company's three pottery lines were lightly used, on the contrary the range of industries using the Lane End line show it to have been well utilized. The Caldon Low line received constant use, with heavy loads of limestone descending from Caldon Low quarries. The difference in costs must be taken as an indication of how heavily that line was used, rather than that the Lane End, Hanley and Burslem lines were lightly used. The maintenance bill for all four of the canal company's plateways was even higher for the financial year ending 25th June, 1831, amounting to £883 4s. 2d. However, the cost in the accounts is grouped under 'Repairs of the Caldon Pottery railways' and so there is unfortunately no breakdown between the two locations as in 1829.[25]

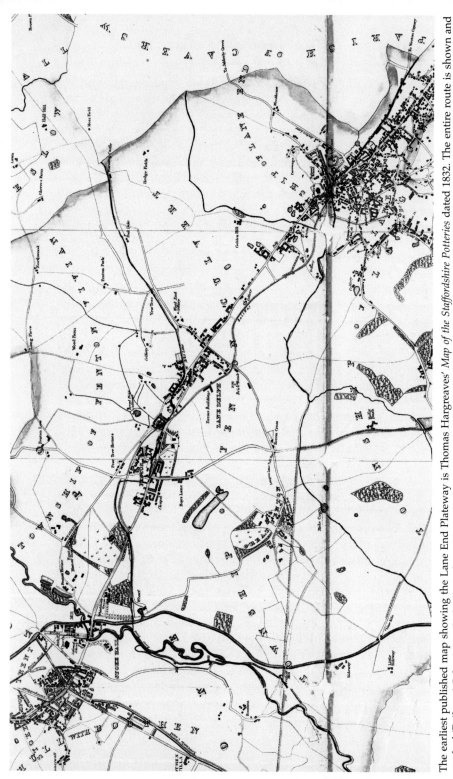

The earliest published map showing the Lane End Plateway is Thomas Hargreaves' *Map of the Staffordshire Potteries* dated 1832. The entire route is shown and marked 'Railway'. It begins at Stoke Basin (*top left*), marked as 'Wharf', and runs all the way to Lane End where it can be seen to split into two branches. Also to be seen is the network of colliery branches north of Fenton which were associated with the Lane End line.

Courtesy of Special Collections and Archives, Keele University Library

CHAPTER EIGHT

Interest by an Early Railway Company

Some evidence of the Lane End line's obvious success and usefulness in its first decade of operation, can be gauged from the great interest displayed in it by the North Stafford Railway Company, not to be confused with the much later North Staffordshire Railway Company. This independent railway company was formed to construct the North Stafford Railway, now sometimes popularly known as the 'Consall Plateway'. This line ran from Consall Forge near the Caldon Canal to Weston Coyney and was built between 1815 and 1819. The railway company thought it desirable that their line should ultimately be connected with the Lane End Plateway, the most easterly point of which was under 1.5 miles distant. Much of the land over which the North Stafford Railway passed belonged to the proprietors of the railway company, although a portion of the planned route belonged to the Marquess of Stafford, whose permission to construct the railway was obtained.[1]

On constructing their Lane End line, the Trent & Mersey Canal Co. did not construct it to the most easterly point permitted by their Act, which was some way east of the centre of Lane End. It is clearly shown by the original survey that the line was authorized as far as a road called 'Mill Field Lane', yet it was only built alongside Market Street as far as Anchor Road, 0.5 miles to the north-west.[2] Mill Field Lane is the very same road which permission was obtained for the North Stafford Railway to be built to, having passed through Lord Stafford's land. A draft of the original lease from the Marquess to the proprietors of the railway company, mentions that the railway was to run from 'Consall Wood...to a place called Mill Field Lane near Lane End'.[3] This can scarcely be coincidental and the authorized end point of the Lane End line evidently dictated a suitable place for the North Stafford Railway to terminate.

The railway company's ultimate ambition was that the canal company should extend the Lane End line so that it would reach the North Stafford Railway. On 29th May, 1815 James Loch, agent to Lord Stafford, wrote individual letters to Thomas Sparrow, William Robinson and James Caldwell, representatives of the canal company.[4] He knew that it would be in the Marquess of Stafford's interest if the proposed railway was continued to Lane End, having passed through his land, and this was the object of his writing. To Thomas Sparrow he wrote:-

A set of Gentlemen...have formed themselves into a company to construct a Railway from Consall Wood to Lane end for the purpose of joining the parliamentary line at the latter place...before however they can make any communication with the parliamentary line which the Grand Trunk Canal Company are authorised to make, it will be necessary for the Company to extend their railway to the extreme point permitted to them by Law. It is to this I have to beg your attention & consideration…if they [the railway company] could have the liberty to connect…with the parliamentary line they propose I understand to bring down stone to the Grand Trunk Canal, in considerable quantities for sale &…also to export a considerable quantity of lime.

On writing to James Caldwell, Loch sought to emphasize that the North Stafford Railway was well worth connecting with, even if it had not initially been worthwhile for the canal company to extend their line beyond Lane End. He pointed out that 'for the Canal Company to complete their railway, the distance required…is very small & the expence cannot therefore be great. It was not completed because it led to no manufactory or coal work[s] which would defray the expence, but I conceive that its junction with the North Stafford Railway would amply & very amply too defray the outlay required for its completion'.

The canal company however, were far from enthusiastic. Since the intended purpose of the new line was primarily the carriage of limestone and lime, a direct link to the Lane End Plateway was not in their best interests. Giving the new railway company access to the canal in Stoke, could seriously undermine their authority as the main supplier of limestone into the Potteries from their quarries at Caldon Low, brought into the towns via the Caldon Canal. The railway company were aware the canal company might feel this way and in his letter to William Robinson, Loch

How rapidly the Lane End line became important to the industries situated between Stoke and Lane End is all too obvious in this newspaper advertisement from the *Staffordshire Advertiser* of 5th January 1805. This is under a year after the railway opened, yet already the line is mentioned as a feature of importance for all three of the first properties listed.

© *The British Library Board and reproduced by permission of the British Newspaper Archive*

Capital Freehold Houses, Potworks, Pews, and Building Situations,
The property of the late Mr. RICHARD MYATT, at Lane End, in the Staffordshire Potteries.

TO BE SOLD BY AUCTION,
By Mr. Cook,
At the White Lion Inn, in Lane End aforesaid, on Wednesday the 30th day of January 1805, at 4 o'clock, either in the following or such other Lots as shall be agreed on at the time of sale, and subject to conditions to be then produced, unless previously disposed of by private treaty.

LOT 1. A Large convenient DWELLING-HOUSE, and Garden, with the Out-buildings, and set of POT-WORKS adjoining, together with the Land to the same belonging, and on which the Manufactory may be very considerably extended, situate at the Folly, in Lane End aforesaid, adjoining the Turnpike Road, and the new Collieries, lately opened there, and within 100 yards of the Railway leading from the Grand Trunk Canal, at Stoke, to Lane End.

LOT 2. A capital set of POT-WORKS, in the Market place, at Lane End, well supplied with Water, in the centre of Extensive Collieries, and adjoining to the Railway aforesaid.
This is a very desirable situation, as well on these as on other occasions.

LOT 3. A very capital, substantial, and newly erected WATER-MILL, called the Folly Mill, for Grinding Flint, and other Articles for Potters use, having 16 feet of head, and fall, and capable of having its Powers increased by an Engine, situated close to Coal, near or adjoining the said Railway, and within 300 yards of Lot 1, between which and the Mill there is a good Road, which crosses the Railway.

LOT 4. A set of POT-WORKS, adjoining the Toll gate, at Lane End, in the occupation of Mr. John Furnifier, and under lease to him for a Term, of which nine years are unexpired, under the clear yearly Rent of 25l.

attempted to convince him that the system would actually be advantageous. He had made enquires the results of which suggested that in summer the Caldon Canal could be choked by a growth of vegetation, whilst in winter ice sometimes made the waterway impassable, thus interrupting traffic. He suggested to Robinson that 'when either of these events occurred the Lane End railway would be used for these purposes and this benefits the Canal Company'.

The canal company remained unconvinced that the scheme would truly benefit them. This feeling had been made clear by 5th June, 1815 when Loch observed 'I am very unwilling to be beat by the Canal Company, yet I am very desirous to give them no real cause of complaint'.[5] The canal company's attitude is understandable, since the commercial interests of the North Stafford Railway Company clearly made it a rival concern. Loch wrote as if the distance to extend the Lane End line was not great and it was only 0.5 miles, but it would still have increased the length of the plateway by 20 per cent. It is reasonable that the canal company did not wish to fund a length of railway, which could have led to a loss of profit, even if they had also gained additional tolls. The canal company's refusal to permit the requested connection meant the North Stafford Railway never progressed past Weston Coyney. The last mile of the line to Mill Field Lane passing through Lord Stafford's land was never built, once it became clear that the canal company were not willing to extend their line. Instead the railway terminated at a roadside wharf. Perhaps if the two lines had been joined, the North Stafford Railway would have been more long-lived, for it had fallen into disuse by 1840.[6]

There is another factor, which could feasibly have forced the canal company to build their line up to Mill Field Lane, even though they would still have been at liberty to refuse connection with the North Stafford Railway. A section in the 1831 Trent & Mersey Canal Act re-enacted the powers for the railway to be constructed in the 'manner as described in the Map or Plan of the same Railway' associated with the 1802 Act. If the Marquess of Stafford requested that the railway must be completed, then it became compulsory for the company 'to make, construct, and complete...the said Railway within Twelve Calendar Months next after they shall be required so to do by Notice in Writing from the said Marquis of the County of Stafford'.[7] This section of the Act was probably inserted at the request of Lord Stafford, for an extension of the Lane End line would have benefitted his estate. If Lord Stafford did request that the railway was completed then this would also have been highly advantageous to the North Stafford Railway. However, the 1831 Act may have come too late for a railway then already in decline. The Marquess of Stafford never appears to have given notice for the Lane End line's completion.

The Lane End line passed to the rear of Longton station. This is the site of that part of the route as it appeared in 1959.   *Courtesy Collection Allan C. Baker*

The route of the plateway to the east of Longton station in 1959. This view is looking east towards Market Street, with Times Square in the distance to the right. To the left is the railway bridge carrying the Stoke to Derby line over King Street, which is still a feature of the town.   *Courtesy Collection Allan C. Baker*

CHAPTER NINE

NSR Ownership, Decline and Closure

The entire Trent & Mersey Canal was purchased by the North Staffordshire Railway in January 1847. The canal company were opposed to the competition which the NSR would pose, and by purchasing the canal such that they controlled both systems, the railway company quashed this opposition. This also meant that the NSR inherited the canal company's four horse-drawn plateways. These lines doubtless appeared rather primitive to a company which was operating standard gauge railways with locomotive-hauled passenger trains by April 1848. In August 1848 the NSR opened a station at Longton, on their line from Stoke to Uttoxeter.[1] This section of standard gauge railway between Stoke and Longton, which carried both goods and passenger traffic, ran approximately parallel to the Lane End Plateway. Given the NSR owned both systems it is perhaps surprising that they continued using the horse-drawn canal plateway at all.

At a meeting of the Trent & Mersey Navigation Traffic Committee in 1855, a letter was read requesting that a bridge crossing the plateway on the Green Dock branch be demolished and replaced by a level crossing. Most roads on the line were crossed by level crossings. The road in question was then called Bridge Street, but is now Heathcote Road. The application was declined since it was felt that 'such an alteration would be detrimental to the interest of the Company'. This comment suggests that at this time the NSR were certainly profiting from the operation of

A 1958 view where the plateway formerly passed behind Longton station. This is now the busy thoroughfare Baths Road.   *Courtesy Collection Allan C. Baker*

In 1973 the trackbed of the Lane End line could still be seen to the south of Longton station. This view is looking east towards the station with the Albion Works in the background.

Courtesy of Grahame Boyes

the Green Dock branch, which was only a small component of the Lane End system. In 1858 a further request was made 'to be allowed to pull down the Bridge which carries Bridge Street over the Longton Tramway'.[2] The application was made by the Chief Bailiff of Longton amongst others, who offered to carry out the work at their own cost. This time the request was granted. Subsequently, the Green Dock branch does not seem to have been used south of Heathcote Road, suggesting a level crossing was never put in place, with the southern end of the branch then falling out of use.

The full line of the plateway is shown clearly as 'Tramway' on the 1st edition 25-inch Ordnance Survey map for the area, surveyed *c*.1879.[3] The plateway is shown to have still been a single track line; the passing places are clearly indicated and were 200-300 feet in length. Interestingly, other than at Manor Street where the rails run across the road, this map shows a gap in the rails at every road. It seems unlikely that there were bridges under these roads. The 1867 Bye-laws mentioned in Chapter five describe the wagon wheels in use at that time like those of an ordinary cart. It seems possible that at the level crossings no rails were in place and the wagons were simply wheeled over the road, without the guidance of any rails.

It was towards the end of the railway's life when it was shown on the *c*.1879 Ordnance Survey map, for the NSR obtained an Act in 1891 in which they were authorized to 'abandon for the purposes of public

This interesting building on the south side of King Street stood alongside the Lane End line at the point it crossed the road. It stood at a peculiar angle to the main road, since it was built parallel to the railway rather than to the road. The Ordnance Survey map of c.1879 shows that there was also a passing place located next to this building, which could originally have been associated with the plateway. Seen here in 1973, the building has now been demolished. *Courtesy of Grahame Boyes*

traffic and discontinue the maintenance of the railway or tramway known as the Lane End Tramway…and the Company may deal with or dispose thereof in such manner and on and subject to such terms and conditions as they might think proper'.[4] Portions of the plateways at Hanley and Burslem, possibly disused, are also marked 'Tramway' on the 1st edition 25-inch Ordnance Survey maps.[5] However, none of the three plateways are marked on the 2nd edition maps re-surveyed in 1898. It is unknown exactly when the Lane End Plateway ceased to operate, but presumably it had been out of use for some time, when Parliamentary authorization was sought to abandon it. It is scarcely surprising that the line ceased to be profitable, given the NSR had begun operating a main line railway parallel to the plateway, within a very short time of acquiring it.

The Ordnance Survey map surveyed c.1879 does not mark the line as then being out of use. In 1873 there were six firms which were eligible for reduced rates for carriage of potters' materials from Stoke, since they maintained plateway sidings connected to their works. Two of these firms were in Foley (the eastern extreme of Fenton) and the other four in Longton.[6] This shows that the full length of the line was then in use. Plateway branches serving various works are also shown on the c.1879

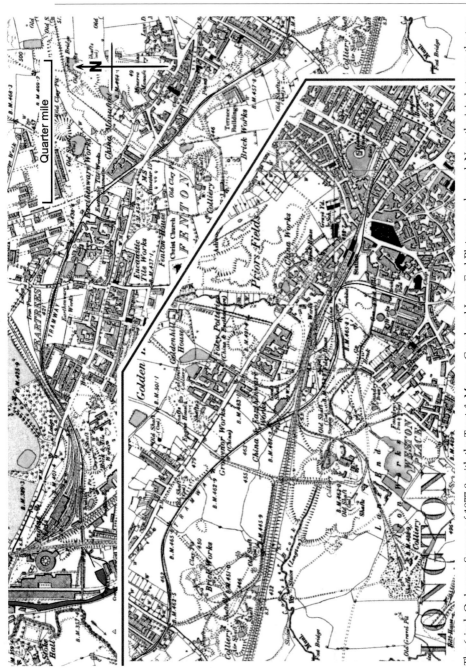

The 6-inch Ordnance Survey of 1877-8 with the Trent & Mersey Canal and Lane End Plateway enhanced. Near the join between the two sections of the map, one of the few private branches which still connected to the plateway is shown. This extensive subsidiary network seems to have served collieries, brickworks and the Lane End Ironworks.
Courtesy of Richard Dean, Canalmaps Archive

Ordnance Survey map. In Fenton a branch passed down the east side of W. Baker & Co.'s earthenware works. Further east and also in Fenton a branch served Oldfield Colliery and Brickworks, before running a considerable distance south to reach further collieries and Lane End Ironworks. To reach the ironworks and associated collieries this branch passed beneath the NSR's line to Derby. The branch at this point became a footpath and later still Bute Street was laid out on the route. Remarkably, the bridge which carried the Derby line over this branch still survives at the end of that road. The Lane End line itself was also

This excellent aerial view dates from 1948 and captures the landscape of Fenton nearly 60 years after the official closure of the Lane End line. The houses visible in the foreground are on Duke Street. The track coming off that road and winding into the distance is the route of the plateway and nowadays is the road known as 'Old Tramway'. The track continues into the foreground, on the opposite side of Duke Street. This preserves the route of a branch line off the plateway which is shown on the Ordnance Survey maps c.1879. The route of the main line ran to the bottom right-hand corner of the photograph having left Duke Street, but in 1948 the route had already been obscured. The spoil heaps of Fenton Colliery are a conspicuous feature and in such an industrialized landscape, it is scarcely surprising that most remains of the plateway have nowadays long since been obliterated.
Courtesy of Britain from Above

This surviving bridge, seen here looking north in 2018, once carried the railway to Derby over a private branch plateway. This branch served Lane End Ironworks and collieries, but must have been disused by the 1890s by which time the Lane End line had already been abandoned.   *Author*

crossed by the NSR line, a little to the east near Longton goods shed. An exchange siding was laid out here, to facilitate the transfer of goods between the two systems. In Lane End there were also short branches connected to two flint mills, one on the Green Dock line and another on the line alongside Market Street. These potters' millers must be some of those firms which were mentioned as having private sidings in 1873.

Use at a later date is implied by an interesting agreement made between Balfour & Co. and the NSR in the latter half of 1884. In this year a siding was built to serve Balfour & Co.'s Oldfield Colliery in Fenton. This siding crossed the Lane End Plateway and a bridge was built over the line in order to keep the route open. The agreement included a sketch of the form this bridge would take, which was constructed of wrought-iron girders supported upon two timber trestles.[7] Since no abandonment Act had yet been passed, the NSR were still under a legal obligation to keep the plateway open at this point. However, the fact that the bridge was constructed seems to suggest some traffic was still using the Lane End line. Another example of the plateway being used in the 1880s demonstrates use by the NSR itself. At a meeting of the NSR Traffic and Finance Committee in April 1883, it was reported that one of the railway company's horses had been injured on the 'Longton Tramway'.[8] The NSR kept horses and had stables in Longton. It is interesting to note that it had its own horses working the line even at this

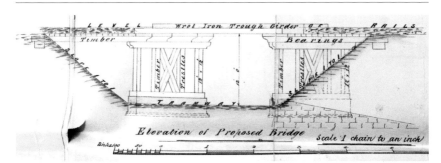

A sketch dated 1884 and showing the constructional details of a bridge proposed to carry Balfour & Co.'s siding to Oldfield Colliery over the plateway. At this time, seven years before the Act authorising the line to be abandoned, the plateway still seems to have been seeing some use.   *Courtesy of The National Archives*

late date. This is the last known evidence of use, only eight years before the Act for abandonment was passed.

The NSR evidently kept the Lane End Plateway open alongside their own line for over 35 years. The plateway was so archaic compared to the railways that company generally operated, that it is surprising they remained loyal to it for so long. The plateway continued in use, for it already had an existing base of customers who maintained their own connections to the line. This was coupled with relatively low maintenance costs, whilst the wagons and horses were generally not owned by the NSR, but by their customers. Overall therefore, the system was a cheap one to keep in operation. The main line railway also served an entirely different market, in that part of its purpose was the carriage of passengers. Ultimately, however, the modern standard gauge railway must have been much more efficient for the haulage of goods, which must be the reason the plateway became obsolete. Since the plateway and modern railway were under the same ownership, they were not in competition with each other, and there was no impetus for the NSR to prolong the plateway's life any longer.

Portions of the railway and its associated infrastructure began to be sold, in the same year as the Act permitting its discontinuation. For example, Messrs Challinor the owner of Fenton Colliery offered to purchase a portion of the tramway in February 1891, before the abandonment Act had even been passed. A month later the NSR accepted an offer of £900 to purchase 'Longton Tramway Cottages'.[9] At a meeting of the Fenton Local Board on 29th September, 1891 the clerk obtained permission to 'purchase from the North Staffordshire Railway Company the portion of the Lane End Tramway between Duke street

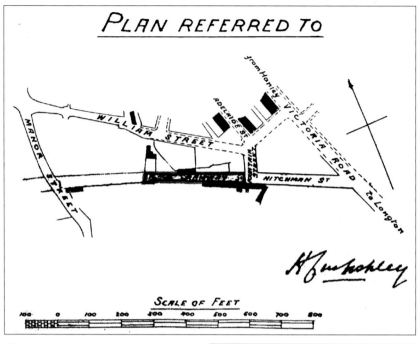

This plan shows the plot of land associated with a conveyance deed dated 1908. The NSR sold Fenton Urban District Council a strip of land which was the trackbed of the plateway. The land in question adjoined Fountain Street in Fenton and was directly opposite Hitchman Street, which had at this time already been built over the plateway route.

Courtesy of John Fendek, James Kent (Ceramic Materials) Ltd.

In 1908, alongside purchasing a section of the plateway trackbed from the NSR, Fenton Urban District Council also purchased an adjoining plot of land from William Baker. This piece of land was described as 'a plot of land fronting Fountain Street and Old Tramway, Fenton' and the former course of the railway was labelled on this plan associated with the deed.

Courtesy of John Fendek, James Kent (Ceramic Materials) Ltd

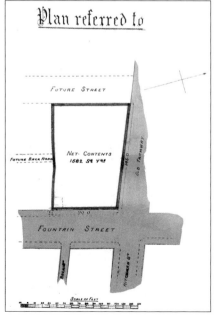

This path leading to Duke Street, seen here probably in the 1950s, can be seen to maintain a fairly level gradient and was the trackbed of the Lane End line. The terraced houses to the left previously stood in Mason Street, Fenton.

Courtesy of Stoke-on-Trent City Archives

and Glebe street'. The price paid for this section of the line was £50.[10] By September 1892, the terminal end of the plateway in Longton was being broken up and the land either sold or leased.[11] The section of the line which diverged to Green Dock was leased to the Corporation of Longton, whilst of the previous section part was sold to the Corporation of Longton and another part to the Duke of Sutherland.[12] A further 'plot of land [which] formed part of a certain railway or tramway known as the Lane End Tramway' was purchased by the Fenton Urban District Council in 1908 for £150. This section adjoined Fountain Street in Fenton (*see page 68*).[13]

Much of the Lane End Plateway's route was evidently sold off by the NSR before the turn of the 20th century. However, despite the whole route from Stoke to Lane End being out of use by the late 1880s, a section of the line survived as a remarkable anomaly into the 20th century. This was the very first section of the plateway, between the wharf at Stoke and the former turnpike road. In 1912 the General Manager of the NSR stated it was still used on a daily basis. Its function at that point was that – 'ordinary waggons and carts use them [plate rails] to get from the canal basin to the high road, a few hundred yards away, the same rate of toll being charged as on the canal'.[14] This is the section of plateway mentioned in Chapter Four. Re-laid at a wider gauge at a late date, parts of it remained substantially intact even in the 1970s. It has now been dismantled and the route forms a metalled track south of City Road, Fenton. This track is private and inaccessible, but no real traces of the railway seem to be visible there today. It is unknown for how much longer after 1912 this section of plateway remained in use. The fact that standard carts could be drawn along a plateway, was a favourable point occasionally expounded by early supporters of plateway technology. However, most plateway wagons were built specifically for railway use. There seems to have been little of the interchanging of carts between plateways and roads, once discussed as a merit of this form of railway.[15] It is therefore intriguing to find the last vestiges of this plateway used in the 20th century, as a mechanism to ease the drawing of 'ordinary carts' to the main road.

The Lane End line is seen alongside Pratts' Sidings signal box *c*.1939. The re-laid section of plateway is here substantially intact compared to later photographs from the 1970s. The colour works of James M. Brown Ltd stood behind the wall to the left of the line and still occupy the same site today.

Courtesy of The Railway & Canal Historical Society, Baxter Collection

This interesting view would seem to date from the early 1950s, when the re-laid section of the Lane End line between City Road and the canal was substantially intact. The locomotive is on the standard gauge line to Stoke Works and running alongside this, the degraded remains of the plateway are still in place. The visible bridge carries the NSR main line to Stone and the photographer's vantage point must have been the bridge carrying the Derby line. *Courtesy of Stoke-on-Trent City Archives*

The remains of the Lane End Plateway looking towards Stoke Works and the canal around 1950. The cambered construction of the horse path is illustrated well by this photograph.
Courtesy of Staffordshire Past Track

Details of the rails and setts which formed the plateway in 1950, probably taken somewhere in the vicinity of City Road.
Courtesy of Staffordshire Past Track

The route of the plateway looking west from City Road in 1972. In the foreground some steel plate rails may be seen *in situ*, partially hidden beneath metalling these continue for some distance. To the right is Pratts' Sidings signal box and the Biddulph Valley line.
Courtesy of Grahame Boyes

CHAPTER TEN

The Legacy of the Lane End Plateway

In 1759, nearly 20 years before the opening of the Trent & Mersey Canal, the ancient route from Newcastle-under-Lyme to Uttoxeter was turnpiked.[1] This turnpiked thoroughfare was a valuable transport link to the potters of Lane End, for the road passed through their town. Indeed, the turnpike's importance can be gauged from the linear nature of Fenton and Longton, settlements which expanded along the road. Also of critical importance to urban expansion, were the coal measures suitable for firing ware, which were crossed by the turnpike in these towns.[2] The opening of the Trent & Mersey Canal further heightened the development of pottery towns such as Lane End. However, since the canal did not pass directly through that town, the turnpike road must have remained the arterial route to Fenton, Longton and Lane End. The completion of the Lane End Plateway in 1804 provided a competing line of communication, which must rapidly have become of equal importance to the turnpike road of 45 years earlier.

Between 1738 and 1801, prior to the opening of the plateway, the population of the towns of Lane End and Longton expanded linearly at around 60 people per annum. After 1801 the population entered another phase of growth, at a constant but much expanded rate. The approximate population of the area in 1801 was 4,000. By 1838 it was nearly 12,000, a rate of population growth of approximately 220 people per annum.[3] This is a decade before the opening of the NSR's main line railway, hence the turnpike road and the plateway were still the pivotal routes to Lane End and Longton. A rapidly expanding population occurred throughout the pottery towns of Staffordshire in this period, so a change in the rate of population expansion is nothing unusual. However, in the case of Lane End and Longton, the rapid acceleration in the rate at which the population grew, must partially be down to the Lane End Plateway. This railway is likely to have had a significant influence on the way these eastern pottery towns grew and developed.[4]

The pottery industry developed later in Lane End than in other Staffordshire pottery towns, yet Longton was home to Staffordshire's first porcelain factory in the mid-18th century. In the early 19th century Lane End rose in prominence and became an important centre for bone china manufacture. There was also a related increase in coal mining here in the same period.[5] Alongside the turnpike road and readily available coal, perhaps one of the main catalysts for the growth of Lane End and Longton was the sale of land in the 1780s by the Heathcote and

Sutherland estates. This opened the towns to development.[6] Supplementing these factors, the Lane End line must have been a valuable secondary catalyst for the industrial expansion of these towns at the start of the 19th century. It ran parallel to the turnpike road, complimenting that earlier route and contributing to the development which took place along it. The plateway became a critical piece of local infrastructure, a vital transport link for a wide range of industries.

The importance of the Lane End, Hanley and Burslem plateways has long been known, in terms of the development of transportation in the Staffordshire Potteries. Yet, these early railways have been little studied and many interesting historical details concerning them remain to be elucidated. Andy Guy has recently highlighted the fact that these railways were unusual in that they served towns and passed through urban neighbourhoods at an early date. In his words – 'The potteries railways exemplify many atypical features…direct lines into and within factories, the mixed nature of the loads, the town depots, and particularly the urban setting'.[7] As the longest of these three plateways, the revenue derived from the Lane End line was probably more than that from the other two, hence it could be said to be the most important of these unusual urban plateways.

As mentioned previously, a colliery plateway at Kidsgrove communicated with the Trent & Mersey Canal as early as 1797. This, however, was an entirely different kind of system, owned by the colliery rather than the canal company and therefore only carrying a very limited range of goods. Since they were owned by the canal company itself and for public use, the Lane End Plateway and its sibling lines carried a wide range of goods, with a variety of different industries including potteries, pottery raw materials manufacturers, collieries and ironworks, all paying tolls to carry their goods over the lines. This plateway has long since been outmoded and very few traces of it exist today, even for those who know where to look. Nonetheless, it played its part in the development of Longton and Fenton as they are today and was the longest railway in the Potteries at a critical point in the expansion of North Staffordshire's famous pottery industry. These facts make this railway worthy of note and its history and contribution to the towns it served should be remembered.

This 1972 view showing the plateway route looks east from beneath the bridge over the Derby line. The Biddulph Valley line can be seen on the left with Pratts' Sidings signal box in the distance. *Courtesy of Grahame Boyes*

The route of the Lane End Plateway here ran alongside the standard gauge line into Stoke Works. The bridges carrying other NSR lines over the horse-drawn route were built with sufficient space for the Stoke Works line which was built later.
Courtesy of Grahame Boyes

REFERENCES

ABBREVIATIONS

CRO – Cheshire Record Office
DRO – Derbyshire Record Office
NLS – National Library of Scotland
PA – Parliamentary Archives
RCHS – Railway and Canal Historical Society
SRO – Staffordshire Record Office
TNA – The National Archives
WSL – William Salt Library

INTRODUCTION

1 Peter Lead, *The Trent & Mersey Canal* (Moorland Publishing, 1980), p. 11

2 H. A. Moisley, 'The Industrial and Urban Development of the North Staffordshire Conurbation', *Transactions and Papers (Institute of British Geographers)*, No. 17 (1951), pp. 154-155

CHAPTER ONE

1 Charles Hadfield, *The Canals of the West Midlands* (David & Charles, 1966), p. 198

2 *Staffordshire Advertiser*, 13 Aug. 1796

3 *Staffordshire Advertiser*, 10 Sept. 1796

4 *Journal of the House of Commons*, Vol. LII (12 July 1796 – 5 Oct. 1797), p. 335

5 SRO, Q/RUm/31 (pt); SRO Q/RUm/19

6 37 Geo. III, *c.*81; PA, HL/PO/PU/1/1797/37G3n206

7 SRO, Q/RUm/20; SRO, Q/RUm/20 (pt)

8 *Staffordshire Advertiser*, 2 Sept. 1797

9 SRO, D6578/10/1

10 Richard Dean, 'Churnet valley conundrums', *Journal of the Railway and Canal Historical Society*, Vol. 39, Pt. 3 (2017), p. 163

11 NLS, MS 19855, ff. 19v.-23

12 Samuel Smiles, *Lives of the Engineers, With an Account of Their Principal Works*, Vol. 2 (John Murray, 1861), pp. 149-150

13 Peter Lead, *The Caldon Canal and Tramroads: Including the Uttoxeter and Leek Canals and the North Stafford Railway* (The Oakwood Press, 1990), p.67

14 *Staffordshire Advertiser*, 6 Sept. 1800

15 SRO, Q/RUm/26-27; SRO Q/RUm, 26 (pt)

16 SRO, Q/RUm/30-32; Q/Rum/27 (pt)

17 *Journal of the House of Commons*, Vol. LVI (29 Oct. 1801 – 28 June 1802), p. 151; 42 Geo. III, c.xxv; SRO, D593/V/3/31

CHAPTER TWO

1 *Staffordshire Advertiser*, 21 Oct. 1801

2 *Staffordshire Advertiser*, 29 Jan. 1803

3 *Staffordshire Advertiser*, 10 Apr. 1802

4 *Staffordshire Advertiser*, 21 Jan. 1804

5 *Staffordshire Advertiser*, 14 July 1804

6 SRO, D593/H/9/6; *Lengths and Levels to Bradshaw's Maps of the Canals, Navigable Rivers, and Railways, in the Principal Part of England* (London, 1833), p. 18

7 WSL, M167

8 Lead, *Trent & Mersey*, pp. 9-10

9 Andy Guy, 'Missing links: some atypical early railways in Britain', in David Gwyn (ed.), *Early Railways 5* (Six Martlets Publishing, 2014), p. 186

10 Robert Copeland, *A Short History of Pottery Raw Materials and the Cheddleton Flint Mill* (Cheddleton Flint Mill Industrial Heritage Trust, 1972), p. 41

11 Guy, 'atypical early railways', pp. 186-7

12 Peter Lead, *Agents of Revolution: John and Thomas Gilbert – Entrepreneurs* (University of Keele, 1989), p. 134 and 172

CHAPTER THREE

1   James Anderson (ed.), 'Minutes to be observed on the construction of rail-ways', *Recreations in Agriculture, Natural-History, Arts, & Miscellaneous Literature*, No. 6 Vol IV (Feb. 1801), pp. 473-477

2   DRO, D5974/3/1, 21 Jan. 1795

3   DRO, D503/41/1, f. 49; R. B. Schofield, *Benjamin Outram 1764-1805* (Merton Priory Press, 2000), pp. 313-316

4   NLS, MS 19876, ff. 19-20

5   NLS, MS 19871, f. 1v.

6   P. J. Riden, 'The Butterley Company and Railway Construction, 1790-1830', *Transport History*, Vol. 6 (1973), p. 34

7   DRO D503/41/1, f. 50

8   J. Lindsay, 'The Butterley Coal and Iron Works, 1792-1816', *Derbyshire Archaeological Journal*, Vol. 85 (1965), p. 34

9   DRO, D503/41/1, f. 111

10 Riden, 'Railway Construction', pp. 40-43

11 Riden, 'Railway Construction', p. 36

12 DRO, D503/41/1, f. 111

13 DRO, D503/41/1, f. 111

14 John Farey, *General View of the Agriculture of Derbyshire*, Vol III (B. McMillan, 1817), p.436

15 C. R. Clinker and Charles Hadfield, 'The Ashby-de-la-Zouch Canal and its Railways', *Transactions of the Leicestershire Archaeological and Historical Society*, Vol. XXXIV (1958), p. 66

16 WSL, M167

17 Cyril Boucher, *John Rennie 1761-1821* (Manchester University Press, 1963), p. 125

18 Lead, *Caldon Canal*, p. 92

CHAPTER FOUR

1   Riden, 'Railway Construction', p. 39

2   Lead, *Caldon Canal*, p. 92

3   Graham Boyes and Brian Lamb, *The Peak Forest Canal and Railway: An Engineering and Business History* (Railway and Canal Historical Society, 2012), pp. 94-95

4   Lead, *Caldon Canal*, p. 92

5   Anderson (ed.), 'Minutes', pp. 475-476

6   R. Patel, 'Early Railway Artefacts in the North Midlands', *Backtrack*, Vol. 29 (2015), p. 7

7   RCHS, Baxter Collection, Box 5

8   Peter Lead, personal communication; Peter Lead, 'Tramroads on the Potteries Coalfield', *Journal of the Staffordshire Industrial Archaeology Society*, No. 5 (1974), pp.6-7; Lead, *Trent & Mersey*, No. 42

CHAPTER FIVE

1   RCHS, Baxter Collection, Box 5; In the 1950s Baxter measured the gauge at 3' 11" on the only section of the line then extant. This section was re-laid at a wider gauge for use with carts. Baxter knew this was not the original gauge as he did not include it in the gazetteer in his *Stone Blocks and Iron Rails*. Peter Lead measured a gauge of 4' here in 1975.

2   Anderson (ed.), 'Minutes', p.476

3   North Staffordshire Railway, *Rules, Bye-laws, Regulations, & Orders, with Reference to the Navigation from the Trent to the Mersey* (Hanley, 1867), p. 9

4   Bertram Baxter, *Stone Blocks and Iron Rails* (David & Charles, 1966), p. 185; A length of stone blocks *in situ* south of

Consall Lane were measured by the author in 2017. The spike holes in each pair of blocks were 48-49 inches apart. Rails at Cheddleton Flint Mill probably originated on this line and are 5" wide with a central notch for the spike. With these rails some 47 inches between spike holes would be expected for 3 feet 6 inch gauge. Given these blocks have spent over 175 years unmaintained they have probably drifted slightly and the measured values are therefore consistent with 3 feet 6 inch gauge.

5   Baxter, *Stone Blocks*, p. 17

6   42 Geo. III, *c.*xxv

7   North Staffordshire Railway, *Regulations, & Orders*, p. 9

8   TNA, RAIL 878/1, 30 May 1854
9   Boyes and Lamb, *Peak Forest Canal*,
    p. 101; David Ripley, *The Little Eaton
    Gangway and Derby Canal* (The
    Oakwood Press, 1993), p. 23; Wheels
    from both these lines can be

examined and measured at the
National Railway Museum.
10 Baxter, *Stone Blocks*, p. 78
11 North Staffordshire Railway,
    Regulations, & Orders, p. 9
12 SRO, Q/RUm/254

CHAPTER SIX

1   SRO, Q/RUm/30-31; 42 Geo. III, *c.*xxv
2   'A survey of lands belonging to the Trent
    and Mersey Canal Company beginning
    at Derwent Mouth and ending at Stone',
    1816, Vol. 2, Sheet XLV-XLVII; The first
    volume of this survey is in the
    Waterways Archive, Ellesmere Port.
    Unfortunately, the second volume of the

original survey has not been successfully
traced. A copy kindly supplied by
Richard Dean of the Canalmaps Archive
is of poor quality, but most features of
interest can be made out.
3   Thomas Hargreaves, *Map of the
    Staffordshire Potteries and Newcastle*
    (Burslem, 1832); SRO D593/H/3/446

CHAPTER SEVEN

1   42 Geo. III, *c.*xxv
2   Farey, *Agriculture of Derbyshire*, p.116;
    SRO, D3098/8/11
3   42 Geo. III, *c.*xxv
4   John Ward, *The Borough of Stoke-upon-
    Trent* (W. Lewis & Son, 1843), p. 387;
    Jean Lindsay, *The Trent & Mersey Canal*
    (David & Charles, 1979) pp. 88-9
5   TNA, RAIL 878/2, Feb.-Apr. 1868 and
    16 Nov. 1867
6   TNA, RAIL 878/2 , 16 Feb. 1872 and
    25 Feb. 1873
7   North Staffordshire Railway, *Rules,
    Bye-Laws, Regulations and Orders of the
    Company of Proprietors of the Navigation
    from the Trent to the Mersey, Made at a
    General Assembly of the said Proprietors ...
    on Wednesday, the 10th Day of April, 1833*
    (Burton-on-Trent, undated), pp. 9-10;
    Regulations, & Orders (1867), pp. 9-10
8   *Staffordshire Advertiser*, 5 Jan. 1805
9   *Staffordshire Advertiser*, 11 Apr. 1812
10 *Staffordshire Advertiser*, 14 July 1818
11 *Staffordshire Advertiser*, 2 Mar. 1811
12 Simon Shaw, *History of the Staffordshire
    Potteries* (Scott Greenwood & Co.,
    1900), p. 60
13 Ward, *Stoke-upon-Trent*, p. 506
14 *Staffordshire Advertiser*, 25 Dec. 1819
15 CRO, QDP 319
16 Canalmaps Archive, NSR contract
    plan for building the Biddulph Valley

Line, *c.*1856
17 Joseph Priestly, *Historical Account of the
    Navigable Rivers, Canals and Railways, of
    Great Britain* (London, 1831), p. 643;
    Diane Baker, *Potworks: The Industrial
    Architecture of the Staffordshire Potteries*
    (RCHM England, 1991), p.56
18 J.H.Y. Briggs, *A History of Longton: I
    The Birth of a Community* (University of
    Keele, 1982), p. 23
19 Lead, 'Tramroads on the Potteries
    Coalfield', *Journal of the Staffordshire
    Industrial Archaeology Society*, No. 5
    (1974), p. 13
20 *Staffordshire Advertiser*, 19 Apr 1806
21 J. Phillips and W. F. Hutchings, *A Map
    of the County of Stafford, Divided into
    Hundreds & Parishes From an accurate
    Survey, Made in the Years 1831 and 1832*
    (Henry Teesdale & Co., 1832)
22 *Reprint of the first edition of the one-inch
    Ordnance Survey of England and Wales:
    Stafford* (David & Charles, 1983)
23 Shaw, *Potteries*, p. 73; Lead,
    'Tramroads', p. 14
24 Stanley H. Beaver, 'The Potteries: A
    Study in the Evolution of a Cultural
    Landscape', *Transactions and Papers
    (Institute of British Geographers)*, No. 34
    (1964), p. 17; Ward, *Stoke-upon-Trent*,
    pp. 573-4
25 SRO, D1798/HM37/19

CHAPTER EIGHT

1 Lead, *Caldon Canal*, pp.85-89
2 SRO, Q/RUm/30, 31 and 32
3 SRO, D593/T/7/1
4 SRO, D593/K/1/5/4, 29 May 1815 (all three letters quoted subsequently)
5 SRO, D593/K/1/5/4, 5 June 1815
6 Lead, *Caldon Canal*, p.92
7 1 William IV, c. lv; PA, HL/PO/PB/1/1831/1W4n91

CHAPTER NINE

1 Rex Christensen and R. W. Miller, *The North Staffordshire Railway* (David & Charles, 1971), pp. 44-45
2 TNA, RAIL 878/2, 5 Oct. 1855 and 16 Mar. 1858
3 Staffordshire 25-inch OS Sheets XVIII.5, XVIII.6 and XVIII.11 (surveyed *c*.1879, published *c*.1880)
4 54-55 Vic., *c*.xxxiv; PA, HL/PO/PB/1/1891/54&55V1n64; 'The North Staffordshire Railway Company to The Fenton Urban District Council, Conveyance...of a plot of land fronting to Fountain Street, Fenton', 30 Oct. 1908, document privately owned
5 Staffordshire 25-inch OS Sheet XII.9 (surveyed 1865-1877, published *c*.1881), Sheet XII.13 (surveyed 1865-1878, published 1879)
6 TNA, RAIL 878/2, 25 Feb. 1873
7 TNA, RAIL 532/19
8 TNA, RAIL 532/149, 3 Apr. 1883
9 TNA, RAIL 532/20, 24 Feb. 1891 and 24 Mar. 1891
10 *Staffordshire Advertiser*, 3 Oct. 1891
11 Tom Foxon, *The Trent & Mersey Canal: Trade and Transport 1770-1970* (Lightmoor Press, 2015), p. 47
12 SRO, D593/H/9/70
13 'Conveyance', 30 Oct. 1908
14 Edwin Pratt, *A History of Inland Transport and Communication in England* (Kegan Paul, 1912), pp. 210-211
15 Baxter, *Stone Blocks*, pp. 46-47

CHAPTER TEN

1 J. G. Jenkins (ed.), *A History of the County of Stafford*, Vol. 8, (Victoria County History, 1963), pp. 1-8
2 Moisley, 'Development', pp. 154-157; Beaver, 'The Potteries', p. 14
3 Ward, *Stoke-upon-Trent*, p. 43
4 Copeland, *Pottery Raw Materials*, p. 3
5 Jenkins (ed.), *History*, p. 238 and 243
6 Baker, *Potworks*, p. 37
7 Guy, 'atypical early railways', p. 188

Looking north along the Trent & Mersey Canal from City Road bridge in 1972. The site of Stoke Basin lies in the opposite direction, some 0.25 miles to the south. The buildings to the right of the canal largely still exist today, and include the former potters' mill of W. J. Dolby Ltd.   *Courtesy of Grahame Boyes*

A 1973 view showing a path at the end of Bute Street, which follows the route of a private branch off the Lane End line. The bridge once carried the NSR Derby line over this branch plateway.   *Courtesy of Grahame Boyes*

INDEX

This index covers both the main text and the illustration captions. Where a page reference is only to an illustration, that number is given in *italics*.

A detailed 1972 view showing the former route of the plateway and line to Stoke Works, where they passed firstly beneath the Derby line, then beneath the main line to Stone.

Courtesy of Grahame Boyes

The route of the Lane End line looking west through Stoke Works towards the canal.

Courtesy of Grahame Boyes